"Sexual addiction is devastating—to the person who is addicted as well as to those who love them. It's a difficult topic to address, but one that has to be met head-on. Secrets must be revealed for healing to occur. If you or someone you care for is struggling with sexual addiction, take hope in Jonathan Daugherty's transparent example."

Jim Daly, President, Focus on the Family

"Finally, a book that poignantly portrays the honest struggles of a man's heart, the desperate cries of his soul, the longings of his hopes and dreams, and the unending grace of the God that saves him. Jonathan gives a step-by-step account of the bondage he experienced as a result of hiding and what it took to find the truth about himself. *Secrets* brings it all into the Light!"

Lee Preston, Director & Counselor, Shadow of His Wings Ministry

"It's no secret. There is always a different kind of credibility, and a different kind of hope, when you hear the words of someone who has been to the dark side and returned. Jonathan Daugherty has been there, but God himself brought him back. If you want hope and insight for your life, a loved one, or your ministry— why not get it from one who has experienced the solution? Why not learn how to escape the death-roll of a life trapped in the chains of secrets? Help is here."

Dr. Fred Lybrand, Senior Pastor, Northeast Bible Church, San Antonio

Secrets

A TRUE STORY OF ADDICTION, INFIDELITY, AND SECOND CHANCES

Jonathan Daugherty

www.newgrowthpress.com

New Growth Press, Greensboro, NC 27404
Copyright © 2008, 2017 by Jonathan Daugherty

Scripture quotations are taken from THE HOLY BIBLE, NEW INTERNATIONAL VERSION®, NIV® Copyright © 1973, 1978, 1984, 2011 by Biblica, Inc.® Used by permission. All rights reserved worldwide.

Cover Design: Tom Temple, tandemcreative.com
Typesetting: Gretchen Logterman

ISBN 978-1-945270-80-2 (Print)
ISBN 978-1-945270-82-6 (eBook)

Library of Congress Cataloging-in-Publication Data on file

Printed in the United States of America

24 23 22 21 20 19 18 17   2 3 4 5

To my wife, Elaine.

You show me that, in spite of my history of keeping secrets, true love conquers all. I love you, and that is no secret.

CONTENTS

Acknowledgments ix

Introduction: A Letter from the Author 1

The Secret 5

Hide 11

Fraud 19

Death 25

High & Low 33

Frustrated Manhood 39

Fuel 47

Conflictions 53

The Light 59

Faking 65

Marriage Works! 73

Stepping Off the Cliff 79

Racing to the Bottom 85

The End . . . Almost 93

Doors 99

Baby Steps 105

Blessings 113

The Final Chapter 121

Appendix 125

Acknowledgments

This book has been my first venture into the world of "real" publishing. In other words, it has been unfamiliar territory. Any journey into the unfamiliar is a scary one, riddled with various degrees of anxiety concerning all the uncertainties ahead. Despite all the unknowns, I am glad I took this journey. My knowledge has been increased and my horizons of dreams expanded. Yet, the journey never would have started (or finished) without the help of some key people along the way.

The seed for the start of this journey was planted in me even as a child because of the value and importance my parents placed on reading. Although I wasn't a heavy reader as a kid, I have grown in my appreciation of the written word over the years. This desire to communicate through words was planted in me by my parents, and I am grateful for their influence.

There isn't nearly enough room in this book (especially in a short little thank-you section) for me to adequately express my appreciation to my wife, Elaine, for all that she has contributed in my life. She has patiently and graciously been my suitable helper through the ups and many downs of our relationship. She has offered valuable insights into the editing and polishing of this manuscript. She has picked me up when I felt down and didn't think this project would ever come to completion. She has cheered for me, challenged me, and comforted me in all of life's adventures. Thank you, Elaine.

I want to thank all my friends who were willing to read through the very rough drafts of this manuscript and for their wise insights offered along the way. Also, my dear friends at our church who encouraged me to keep pressing on, never allowing me to believe this wasn't a story that needed to be told.

A very special thank you to Jeff Gerke for his insightful editing. Jeff, I appreciate your honesty and uncompromising integrity in telling me like it is.

Finally, I want to thank God for mercifully bringing me to a point in my life where I could tell the story, no longer bound by the shame of my past. I thank him for giving me the ability and desire to write. I pray I use these gifts in a manner that brings others to a point of brokenness and surrender, a place where they can know Life.

I am glad I stepped into the unfamiliar. I hope all who read this book will gain that same courage.

Introduction:
A Letter from the Author

Dear Reader, I know we haven't met, but I hope we can become friends—fast. The reason we ought to become friends is because what I have written in this book isn't really for strangers. It is the kind of information one might only feel comfortable sharing with a close, personal friend. So, let's be friends, OK?

I wrote this book for two main reasons. First, I wanted to share the many secrets I have kept over the years and uncover how they got there and why I hid them. I think we all keep secrets, but we don't always know how they got there and why we keep choosing to cover them up. By sharing my story my hope is that it will help you understand yourself better, thus encouraging you to bravely enter those dark corners of your soul that have grown musty and stale from years of untouched secrets.

The second reason I wrote this book was to invite you to embark on a new journey, a new life that doesn't hide who you really are. We are all prone to want to hide, whether it is something "small" like having a crush on someone in high school or something "big" like lying to your spouse about an affair, pornography, or cheating on your taxes (yes, I consider that a big one). But by keeping secrets our lives tend to drift off course. We hide our flaws and overly accentuate our strengths, believing this will enhance our lives and relationships. Yet in doing so we never find true, lasting fulfillment. That is why I want to invite you to a new direction in life, one that is not always comfortable or fun, but does provide opportunity for experiencing true contentment and peace.

This book is very personal, maybe too personal. But I wrote it this way on purpose. I want you to see how bumpy, jagged, and unpredictable my life has been—just like yours.

I want you to know that you are not alone on this journey called life. I want to embolden you to reach in and deal with the pain and confusion in your life, to reach up and connect with the Lover of your soul, and eventually to reach out and share who you really are with those you love, those who need to know the real you.

This book is not a "teaching book" *per se*, although I am sure there will be nuggets of insight you gain along the way (like the truth that keeping secrets hinders your ability to connect with others on an emotionally significant level). In fact, I have included at the end of each chapter a short segment entitled *Living in the Light* that will share relevant teachable points designed to encourage and equip you in uncovering your own secrets so that you might live free from them.

But beyond these helpful teaching points, I like to think of this book as more of a "story book," simply inviting you to peek in on the story of my life, in hopes that such a viewing might light a spark in your own heart to live from this moment forward with no more regrets. I really want to inspire you to embrace life and live it richly, not bound by secrets, perfectionism, or sin.

One other note about this book that you might need to know is that, while I deal with many "heavy" topics (i.e. pornography, addiction, betrayal, lying, death, etc.), I do not lose my sense of humor, albeit a somewhat dry, sarcastic wit. I hope this doesn't offend you, but instead provides an appropriate balance to dealing with some of life's most difficult circumstances and events. Just thought you should know this before you dive in. I am glad we are friends (that really was fast!). Now you can read my book.

No more secrets,
Jonathan

(By the way, my birthday is March 7th . . . and I *love* chocolate.)

The Secret

I wish it never happened. I remember the day very well. It was 1986 and I was twelve years old. A friend and I were playing in the woods behind his house. It was a hot, steamy summer day. We were pretending to be Rambo, saving captive villagers and waxing the enemy. It felt like boyhood innocence at its best. Then it happened.

"Hey, Jonathan, are you thirsty?" "You bet I am."

We headed off through the woods, back toward my friend's house. We swung our play rifles by our sides, kicking rocks along the way, heading from one point to another in a zigzag manner as adolescent boys are prone to do. My friend was walking a few paces in front of me when he suddenly stopped, turned around, and with an expression on his face like he just calculated the square root of pi, said, "Oh, I just remembered something I wanted to show you."

At that, we changed direction and began marching out into an open field covered with tall alfalfa grass. I still remember the musty smell of that grass, so thick I felt as if I could choke on it in the air. The grass coarsely slapped at our jeans as we waded our way out into the field. I remember how hot it was as we walked out from under the cover of the trees. I felt the sun beat down on my neck and sizzle the beads of sweat as they formed there.

As soon as we entered the field, my friend picked up the pace of his walking. I, however, maintained my slower pace, content to take my time, not thinking there should be any hurry to what we were going to do—whatever that might be.

As my friend went on ahead I could see that he was walking toward a tree stump in the middle of the field. My innocent mind began to imagine what "treasures" that stump might hold. Maybe it contained the carcass of a raccoon or wild dog. Or maybe there was some hidden jewelry or other loot left by Gypsies. (Sure, Gypsies in central Texas. Who knew? This is the way my twelve-year-old mind worked.) Nonetheless, I simply kept walking where my friend was leading.

My friend reached the tree stump first and turned to make sure I was still following. He waited eagerly for me at the stump, and as I got closer I noticed a wry smile stretch across his face. I thought nothing of it, but when I reached him I did get more excited as I anticipated the unveiling of the hidden treasure that lie beneath the stump.

"Are you ready?"

"Sure, I guess. Ready for what?" I said. "Ready for this?"

My friend reached his hand down into the tree stump, feeling around for something. All I could hear was what sounded like dry leaves crackling. Then, triumphantly, he lifted his hand out of the stump, grasping what looked like a tube of glossy paper. I couldn't quite make out what it was. It appeared like it might be a magazine or binder of some sort. He turned toward me, stretched out the cylinder, and opened what he held.

******

There have been moments in my life that have attempted to define me as a person, either positively or negatively. I couldn't always see these moments coming. They just seemed to "appear" without warning. And when such a moment arrived, if I was unprepared to deal with it, I simply got swallowed by it. And, thus, the moment changed me, or at the very least changed my direction. In the case of what I encountered in that open field, my direction was certainly going to be changed.

I am sure my friend had no idea that what he was doing would impact my life the way it eventually did. He never could have imagined in that instant how this seemingly ignorable moment in history would obsessively drive my life for the following thirteen years. Moments do matter. And some matter more than others. This moment crippled me in ways I couldn't realize at the time.

In order to understand the magnitude of this moment, I need to share an incident from earlier in my life. I was six years old. My family was visiting my mom's parents. I loved my Granny's house. It always smelled good, like something sweet was around every corner (except the bathrooms, where it always smelled like old people).

One day I was playing in the corner of the living room while my parents and grandparents were talking. I don't remember what toys I was playing with, but I remember becoming interested in the grown-up conversation on the other side of the room.

"Heaven."

"Hell."

"Sin."

"Jesus."

These were the words I heard as they talked. Periodically, I would toss a question their way, not so they would direct their attention toward me, but so I could understand this story they were telling. What they said sounded so real, so attractive. They spoke of all the bad things people did, and called this sin. They talked about God loving us, his precious creation. They shared how God's heart broke because of our sin, but that he had a plan to fix it. The plan was Jesus paying the penalty we deserved for our sin by dying on a cross and coming back to life. Then they explained how anyone who believed in Jesus would live forever in heaven. I wanted in!

Without drawing attention to myself, I slipped out of the living room and hurried down the hallway. I darted into the bathroom and locked the door behind me. My heart was beating fast, I was nervous about talking to God. But I wanted to go to heaven. I wanted all my wrongs to be covered. I walked over to the toilet and knelt down. With my left arm draped over the toilet seat and my head bowed just below the rim, I prayed.

"God, this is Jonathan. I know I do bad things that you don't like. I heard my parents talking about the plan you made to fix my bad stuff. I don't want to go to hell for being bad. I believe Jesus died for all the bad I've done. Will you save me?"

Nothing happened. My heartbeat did slow down a bit, but I didn't see angels or hear voices. The only sound was coming from water slowly dripping in the toilet. I then realized where I was, the smell of old people jolting me back into the moment. I unlocked the door, walked back down the hallway to the living room, and continued playing in the corner. I had no idea of the significance of my seemingly inconsequential moment in the bathroom. I didn't realize I had just become the newest citizen of heaven.

For several weeks after my bathroom conversion, I prayed every night for Jesus to save me. I kept thinking that I was doing something wrong. I just knew I was supposed to *feel* something. But each time I prayed, I didn't experience anything out of the ordinary. I eventually told my parents what I had done and they were very excited for me, smiles from ear to ear. This helped me feel better. After all, I didn't figure they would be that excited if I had "done it wrong."

If there was anything I did notice change, it was my awareness of right and wrong. It seemed I became more sensitive in recognizing when something was wrong, like there was an internal nudge or twinge when something in life wasn't lining up quite right. While I didn't recognize it immediately, or even know that it had anything to do with what happened in my Granny's bathroom, it was there.

And it was this change that caused the moment with my friend in that field as a twelve-year-old kid to leave such an indelible mark on my life.

******

Pornography.

That is what my friend pulled from the tree stump and so gleefully presented to me. "Pretty cool, huh?" my friend beamed.

I thought my heart stopped when he cracked open those pages. The image printed on that first page I saw was immediately seared into my brain. It is still locked away in the dark recesses of my mind, and could probably be recalled if I chose to pull it up again. I had never seen anything like it, and it caused some very strange reactions in me. Immediately upon seeing the porn I felt the urge to look over my shoulder, as if I knew I was getting away with something. Guilt seemed to spring to life in me and push me toward a "run for the hills" response. But I didn't run. I stared. I wanted to look, even as the guilt pounded at my mind. I felt a rush course through my body that felt amazing, exciting, and arousing (even though I didn't know what that meant at the time). What my body was feeling quickly overpowered any sense of guilt I had, and I craved seeing more.

"Yeah, pretty cool," was all I could utter in response to my friend's question.

We thumbed through the magazine for another few minutes, trying to make out images on some pages that had been rained on. I tried to play it cool, responding to the pictures by taking cues from my friend since this was all new territory for me. But what I really wanted to do was shout Holy cow! This is the wildest feeling I have ever had! My head is spinning, and I'm teetering on the line between vomiting and ecstasy, but this is amazing. How can I reproduce this rush tomorrow and the next day? Instead, I coolly nodded my head, giggled when my friend did, and focused on keeping my jaw from dropping too closely to the ground.

Eventually, my friend rolled up the magazine and stuffed it back down inside the tree stump for some other neighborhood kids to find. We then began to walk away from the stump, through the field, heading in the direction of his house for something to drink. But I wasn't the same. Something had changed. As we marched off that field, I was oblivious to the grass brushing against my jeans or the sun scorching my neck. Instead, my mind was spinning with the naked images I had just seen. In that moment, innocence had been lost. A door to another place had been opened and I had walked through it. I possessed something I did not have before: a secret. And it was a big one.

I wish it never happened.

Living in the Light

What have you experienced in your life that you regret? Is there something that remains hidden, something that happened that frightened you or hurt you? Is there anything that you have gone through in your life where you say today, "I wish it never happened?"

The fundamental first step to living life "in the light" is to acknowledge and confess those things that remain in the dark. I invite you to spend some time conducting a "historical inventory" of your life, maybe even journaling some of your secrets and the experiences you faced. Then, in the presence of a trusted friend, family member, counselor, or clergyman, share your story.

You don't have to share it all at once, but the journey to a life of no more regrets starts by bringing to light what has been in the dark. You can do this!

Hide

My secret changed me. It opened a doorway inside me to a place I didn't know I possessed, a place filled with lust, selfishness, and unquenchable cravings. I started to see the world differently. Girls were no longer innocent, friendly classmates I played with during recess at school, but rather they became like new, blank canvases for my own mental exploration. My imagination ran wild about what wonders lay beneath their clothing. The secret ushered me into a dark, inner world that I never knew existed. A new world of hidden, lustful thoughts.

******

I don't know any twelve-year-old who can adequately process an encounter with pornography. It is traumatic, confusing, exhilarating, and overwhelming. It subtly, and sometimes not so subtly, plants a seed of darkness in the soul. This is not an easy encounter for a child. Most adults can't even manage their sexual feelings very well, so how can a kid be expected to? All I knew to do with my newfound sexual feelings was to hide them. The act of hiding became the diseased root of my relational paradigm. I would mask my sexual feelings and questions and hope that nobody could tell that they were swirling about madly inside my hormone-laced mind. Eventually, in the years to come, hiding any uncomfortable or confusing emotion became the norm for me.

But I couldn't fully process my fateful introduction to pornography that occurred in that empty field. I felt cornered by my secret. The traumatic encounter with porn befuddled me. Why couldn't I handle it? What was it about the porn that stirred me up that day? How could that single exposure hook me so deeply? I had no sufficient answers for any of my questions.

I wasn't expecting naked women to be hidden away in a hollow old tree stump in the middle of a grassy field. My mind wasn't ready for that. It was as if my body had responded to the images without consulting my brain. I felt betrayed by myself, like body and mind somehow disconnected during that encounter and now sexual urges were running my life rather than reason or common sense. Where could I find answers for my growing confusion and frustration? What could I do with this "splitting" of my insides? Hide.

My hiding, however, wasn't intentional. It just happened that way. This can make sense if you step into the mind of a twelve-year-old. What does that world consist of? A very short history, unparalleled curiosity and the moment at hand. That pretty much sums it up. Any real discussion of future is minimal and hazy at best. In my twelve-year-old mind I could not project into my future the effects my decisions in the present would have. I wouldn't conclude there could be ramifications years down the road unless there was an effect that occurred sixty seconds after a decision I made in the present. So, my "decision" to hide the secret of my encounter with pornography wasn't because I was stupid or lacked judgment. I simply had the mind of a kid. The truth be told, hiding wasn't even really a decision. It was more like just doing what felt natural to do, and isn't that the way it always is with sin?

Hiding comes naturally to us all, doesn't it? When we encounter something we feel incapable of handling, our initial response is to hide, to run, to retreat. Think back in your own life. Didn't you hide certain events and experiences you had in your life because you just didn't know how to respond or what to do with the information that was presented to you? It's a natural response, even if it isn't a healthy one.

But hiding my encounter with porn did not close the door on my new sexual feelings. They had awakened and wanted to be satisfied. Naturally, I began my search in the safest place I could think of: my house. I looked everywhere, trying to find material to answer the call of my budding sexuality. I sneaked through my dad's sock drawer. Nothing. I rummaged through the top shelf in my parent's closet. No porn. I even went through every square inch of the attic, the barn, and the garage. Not one page or picture of pornography. I wish I could say I was proud of my dad for doing his duty as the protector of our home and not allowing such poisonous material inside. But I wasn't proud. I was frustrated and confused, even angry.

I also became afraid that I might be a freak because of this new fascination with pornography. Maybe these sexual feelings were abnormal and I was turning into some kind of pervert (whatever that meant). My dad was a guy just like me, but he didn't appear to be obsessed with sexual things the way I was. Did that mean that he was normal and I wasn't? Was every other guy on the planet able to look at porn only once or just a few times and not get hooked like I did? I became quite afraid of the possible label of "abnormal," so I stuffed these thoughts even deeper into the shadows of my mind, hoping they would just work themselves out over time.

I also became very afraid of getting caught in my search for sexual material. Even though there wasn't any outright pornography in our house, there were clothing catalogs. These catalogs had several pages of lingerie ads, worn by very attractive models (looking back I realize this was my first lesson in fantasy—it never matches real life). I would secretly steal away moments alone in my room with these models, creating all sorts of fantasies. Not all my fantasies at that point in my life were of intercourse or sexual touching. (I was still very naïve regarding the "mechanics" of sex.) Many were fantasies of love, romance, and me being wanted by a beautiful woman. This was the beginning of my "other" world, fantasies that would prove to be a place of pseudo-comfort and escape for years to come. I soon discovered masturbation during these "encounters" with the lingerie models. This self-exploration only intensified my fantasies and lust for more moments alone to engage this growing world of pleasure. At the time I didn't realize it, but I was gradually becoming addicted to the chase, capture, and conquest that is fundamental to the cycle of sexual addiction. I was laying a foundation (more like a house of cards) of building block behaviors that would ultimately topple my life.

I used to stash a few pages from the catalogs behind the headboard on my waterbed. I was very secretive about my sexual feelings and certainly told no one about the catalogs or my use of them. The fears, however, only grew. I would find myself periodically in a mild state of panic, wondering what would happen if my mom found those pages behind my bed. How would I explain such a thing to her? What would my excuse be to Daddy? I began to formulate "escape strategies" for such possibilities of being found out, rehearsing elaborate imaginary conversations in my head that would untangle me from this spreading web of deception. My mind was ever escalating with thoughts that were not part of reality, but rather existed only in this new world of fantasy.

It didn't take long for me to become a divided person. The secret split me down the middle. I was not who I appeared to be. I had to lie to keep the secret alive. I had to create a separate, hidden me in order not to appear as if anything had changed, or was changing. I became skillful at masking true emotions and replacing them with other, "fake" emotions that might appease those asking.

"Jonathan, you look distracted and distant. Are you OK? Do you want to talk about it?"

"No, I'm fine. I'm just tired. We had a tough basketball practice today."

"OK."

It was like a game to me, this hiding and lying, yet I wasn't consciously aware I was playing. And I certainly didn't know of the dangers this game would cause. Or that no one wins at this game. But I would eventually find out that hiding only leads to fear, and fear brings many losses.

******

Everyone has experienced trauma in childhood, an event or set of events that are too overwhelming to process. I faced a traumatic event as a young kid in junior high school that was beyond my capacity to handle. Our school building was old and had restrooms that were actually positioned along a covered outdoor sidewalk connecting two of the buildings. One day during class I needed to use the bathroom so I asked the teacher for a hall pass, which was granted. I exited the classroom, walked down the hallway, pushed open the door to the outside, and spun the hall pass in my hand as I headed toward the boys restroom. I grabbed the handle on the restroom door and flung it open.

Trauma does not announce when it will occur, it just happens. Your system is overwhelmed by the event and you don't know how to proceed. I suppose if trauma did make announcements prior to its arrival, it would no longer be considered trauma because you could prepare for it. Nevertheless, trauma is not pleasant.

I froze in the doorway of the restroom. I witnessed something I couldn't explain or even understand. There were two male special education students in the middle of the room with their pants around their ankles exchanging sexual touch. I immediately lost any urge to use the facilities. I quickly closed the door and ran back toward the school building, but both students had turned and caught a glimpse of me before I was able to shut the door. I was scared, confused, disgusted, and embarrassed. I had been introduced to information I didn't want to process, nor felt capable of processing.

My shock and horror must have been evident when I returned to the classroom because there was this collective gasp from the students and teacher when I walked in. My face was pale, ashen. The teacher got up from her desk, took the hall pass from my hand, and gently guided me out into the hallway where she asked me what happened. I simply told her I saw two special ed students in the bathroom, but refused to divulge any details. I was quietly led to the principal's office where I waited for the director of special education to come meet with me. I sat in that principal's office feeling terrified and horribly uncomfortable. Oh, how I wanted to hide!

When the special ed teacher arrived, we went into another room and sat down, just the two of us. I was then asked to describe, in detail, what I saw in the bathroom. It was an awful experience. I felt as if I had been traumatized twice, once for the "live" incident, and a second time for having to relay the information to an adult I was very uncomfortable talking to. Just to say the word "erection" to the teacher sent hot flashes of embarrassment up my neck and face.

Finally, the interrogation was over and I was allowed to return to class, with yet additional baggage and scars. I slid down into my chair, began doing my schoolwork, yet unable to erase the terrible scene from my mind. No matter how much

I wanted to hide I was unable to escape the realities that were shaping my sexuality. I feared that one day I would have to face this dark trauma in order to lift its imprint from my soul. I just knew that day wouldn't be coming anytime soon.

Living in the Light

Have you felt incapable of handling some of your secrets? That's OK. Don't beat yourself up. We have all experienced trauma, deep wounds that left scars and remain tender to the touch, even now. But be careful of falsely assuming that the secrets you carry are the only things at fault for the dysfunction you may experience today in your relationships or work or faith or whatever else that is askew in your life. Trauma can also play a big part in shaping how you see life and relationships.

Because of this, I think it is healthy to consult with a professional counselor regarding unresolved trauma. I still seek help from counselors from time to time (don't let that discourage you; most really good counselors even see a professional periodically). The key is that you don't have to face life alone, unable to make sense of the things that happened in your past that you couldn't interpret or handle emotionally. You can find resolution, hope, and healing. So, start your search for a good counselor today (you can see the appendix at the back of this book for help).

Don't hide anymore.

Fraud

Dividedness filled my life, not just the hiding of my growing sexual secrets. I learned to compartmentalize everything, to keep everyone at bay through lying or manipulation. It wasn't blatant or obvious, but rather smooth and subtle. The point, I guess, was to keep from having to own up to my budding depravity, my growing self-centeredness. No one likes to admit their inner dysfunctions, their hidden darkness. I obsessively tried to make sure I did everything right, or at least acceptable to those watching. I felt the need to present myself in the way others expected in order not to draw attention to my deficiencies; perfect image on the outside, increasingly rotten reality on the inside.

I remember one instance as a young teenager when a friend and I were playing in his backyard. I had a BB gun and I was just shooting different things out in the greenbelt behind his house. Then, without even thinking, I swung around and pointed the gun at my friend who was about thirty feet away and shot him. The BB hit him in the chest and must have stung pretty good because he let out a yelp like a kicked dog. He sprinted to his back door, flung it open, and wailed to his parents of the evil his friend had just inflicted on him. I actually didn't catch the whole conversation because I bolted through the woods toward my house. I hid.

My immediate reaction to the dark cruelty of my heart being exposed was to hit the trail and find a good hideout. It wasn't that I would deny shooting my friend, just that I didn't want it to appear that this unkindness was characteristic of me as a person. I wanted to make sure that foremost in other people's minds was that I was a great kid, kind and likeable. So, I felt the only thing I could do in response to shooting my friend was to run into the woods and hide, hoping this would cover up my sin.

When I eventually did wander home I was met by my parents, who were both wearing similar scowls on their faces, evidence of their mutual disappointment. My friend's parents had called while I was hunkered down in the woods pleading with God to "make it go away." My parents sat me down and laid out in detail the course of my pending apology to my friend. They went on to inform me that I would also be apologizing to my friend's parents. This terrified me because I was quite afraid of this particular friend's dad. He actually was a nice guy, but to my prepubescent mind he seemed quirky and odd, with a twitch. I dreaded having to "confess my sin" to that man. I longed to hide, to keep my failure (and the inner cruelty behind it) tucked away where I wouldn't be held accountable for it.

This is a fundamental deception for those who carry secrets and think they can simultaneously live in deep, connected relationships. We somehow come to believe that we can move forward in our relationships without ever coming clean about our secrets, like if we just "start over" from here without accepting responsibility for our junk then everything will be fine. It is a big lie that I wouldn't face up to until more than a decade later.

My parents followed through and I apologized to my friend and his parents the next day. But rather than producing the desired effect of me seeing the benefit and wisdom in owning up to my sin and making amends, the encounter drove me further away from such a healthy outlook and instead caused me to dig my heels in deeper in my dividedness. I was committed more than ever to becoming skilled at the art of deception and manipulation, so as to avoid future confessions like this one. In other words, I set my heart more intently on becoming better at hiding, and thus embracing the lie that I could "have my cake (secrets) and eat it too."

Pride is at the root of all sin, all darkness, everything evil. It always leads us toward the dark, toward secrets. My pride was expressing itself through quiet rebellion; a redirecting of my inner person toward all that I believed was proper and right. I wanted to call the shots, do things my way, and this certainly meant avoiding and hiding the uncomfortable moments of my life and instead seeking all that was pleasurable. Funny how our culture promotes the pathway to happiness as being marked by pleasure without pain, not aware that true happiness is only found in a surrendered life, a life of faith in God. Pride truly is at the root of sin, and unhappiness.

******

Strangely enough, I discovered that this game of deception, hiding my inner secrets, seemed to work in my favor when it came to impressing girls. I found there was a certain charm exuded when I presented myself as mysterious, even conflicted. Add a sprinkle of humor and a dash of wit and the formula was complete. And when you stirred in my awakening, and curious, sexuality you wound up with a very combustible, and emotionally shallow, adolescent with a growing number of interested females. And not a clue what was being produced.

What seems so easy to recognize and explain now was not present in my conscious mind as a teenager. I wasn't considering how these "ingredients" were adding up to an emotionally lethal mixture. I was simply following the path of least resistance. And when carrying a secret like pornography, masturbation, and fantasy, that path leads to lying and masking emotions.

My dividedness made it very difficult for me to be direct with anyone. I always felt the need to skirt around deeper, honest issues or struggles. I would joke or be sarcastic to deflect attention away from what I thought might be a glaring weakness in me. Or I would avoid conflict just so I wouldn't face the possibility of rejection or ridicule. All this, however, was happening on a subconscious level in me; I simply wasn't actively aware of these subtle attitudes growing inside me.

As my sexuality blossomed, my skill at subtle, manipulative charm increased. At first, I really wasn't interested in "catching" any girls. The chase was enough. The idea that a girl was interested in me, flirting with me, that was enough. In my mind, that was the catch. The fact that a girl might go out of her way to say hi or glance several times in my direction, that satisfied my desire for being wanted. Looking back, I honestly don't know what I might have done as a young teenager if I had ever actually "caught" one of the girls. Maybe I was afraid or ignorant, just like every other teenage guy out there. I don't know.

I did, however, have a crush on one girl in the sixth grade. It wasn't a sexual crush, it was a true, heartfelt star-in-the-eyes crush. Let's call her Grace, since I don't want to reveal her true identity.

Grace was the kind of girl that made your heart beat faster when she walked by and caused your palms to sweat when she talked to you. I would watch Grace from afar, mesmerized by her beauty and, well, grace. I knew Grace wasn't the kind of girl you could just walk up to and blab about your life and problems and fears. At least that is what I told myself. I was convinced I could only get as close to Grace as my mind would take me. In other words, I rarely talked to Grace. But when I did, I made sure I was exercising all my skills of charm, deceit, and manipulation (subconsciously, of course). I worked hard to present myself to Grace exactly as I thought she expected me to be. Now, before you think too highly of yourself, let's be honest with one another. We have all tried to impress someone, whether romantically, athletically, academically or otherwise, by masking our deficiencies to appear better than we are. This is human nature, and is not easily overcome. I wanted Grace to see all the good in me and none of the bad, to meet all her expectations of a "good guy." This is natural, just not healthy or realistic.

There is a fundamental flaw, however, in trying to present yourself as you believe others expect you to be. What is the flaw? You can't know what others expect unless they tell you! My divided nature led me to all sorts of delusional thoughts concerning other people and their expectations of me. I would formulate what I believed a person expected of me without ever talking to them. And out of that delusion I would engage in my relationship with them, if you call that a relationship. I did this with Grace.

Needless to say, my interactions with Grace were very shallow and never led to any sort of genuine, close friendship. Why? I was talking with someone I created in my mind based on my delusions about what I thought Grace expected of me. I wasn't actually present in the moment with the real Grace standing right in front of me. This is the dirty little secret of dividedness; it leads you to mix fantasy with reality until you can't tell the difference. If you do that long enough, you will end up like I did, a fraud.

Living in the Light

Pride really is at the root of all sin. But it often morphs over time into a characteristic we tend to uphold as valued and honorable in our culture: perfectionism. Do you present yourself to others as someone different from who you really are? Do you speak of your skills or strengths out of proportion to what they are in reality? What about your weaknesses, are you honest about those?

Perfectionism is more about presentation than it is about substance. It demands that the image is perfect, regardless of the fact that the substance is flawed or broken. If you want to live in the light and with no more regrets, you must deal aggressively with this root of perfectionism. It is a tough root to dig up, but persist in your efforts to kill it. You can't live in the light if you don't.

Death

I am going to skip over a few years in my story. You won't miss them, I promise. From ages twelve to seventeen not much happened that isn't common to every kid of those ages. The only significant fact you need to know is that during those years I improved my skill of lying to cover my increasing inventory of secrets. My inner dividedness widened and I began mastering the art of appearing to have it all together, despite the reality that I was growing more confused and frustrated by the day. (But the perfect smile on my face would have fooled you.)

My senior year in high school, though, brings back many fond memories. While I did have a lot of secrets that eventually led to much sorrow in my adult life, I also had many moments and seasons of great fun and enjoyment during my adolescent years. And my senior year was one of those enjoyable seasons—mostly. That final year of high school would introduce a new type of poison to my emotional and spiritual growth, one that was almost too much to bear.

In that year I was coming into my own as an all-star athlete, one of the top basketball players in the state of Texas. I worked hard on my game, and as my skills improved I gained more attention, much more attention. Newspaper columns were written, invitations to all-star games were offered, and stories of some of my games were beginning to be blown out of proportion, much like the fisherman whose two-pound bass grows to ten pounds in a matter of months. Along with this new notoriety came the attention of a lot of girls. And I wasn't complaining.

Despite all the female attention, I wasn't like a lot of the other kids in my school, the ones who felt the natural compulsion to date the first person who showed a slight interest in them and wasn't a total dog (sorry, just the facts of high school immaturity). I never really dated anyone during that year. I was content to bask in the attention of many girls, spreading my "charm" as it were, rather than locking on to only one girl and thus being forced to ignore all others. Just like my attitude toward scoring on the basketball court, I believed more was better. Therefore, I soaked up the attention and attempted to keep all satisfied through quick wit and humor. It seemed to work.

But I couldn't shake increasing feelings of loneliness throughout my final year in high school. In the quiet moments, when I was alone, I would feel powerful twinges of sadness over my inability to truly connect with anyone around me. I held them all at arm's length through my duplicitous lifestyle, and it seemed my arms were growing longer by the minute. I was forming a sort of emotional "bubble" around me so as not to let anyone close enough to catch a whiff of the rotten secrets that were piling up in the landfill of my heart. This distance seemed to create an ache, a loneliness that I couldn't shake. I wasn't aware of it at the time, but I realize now that my aching was God's gentle warning to me of the dangers of living life in selfish isolation. Despite all the wonderful memories from that senior year, my life was subtly setting adrift in a sea with no land on the horizon.

******

Josh (not his real name) was full of life. He was a fun guy with a great sense of humor and knew how to bring a smile to anyone's face. He was a grade or two behind me in school, but never had a problem with making friends of any age. I ran with him in cross country in preparation for the basketball season. (I didn't play football—cardinal sin in Texas—so I was required to participate in cross country practices instead.) Josh and I formed a friendship and we would hang out periodically at school during lunch or other break times.

I secretly envied Josh. Connecting with people seemed so easy, so effortless for him. He could talk to anyone and not seem self-conscious or inhibited. I admired him for this. I always felt awkward in social situations where there weren't clearly defined rules or boundaries. I never felt free to just fire up a conversation with a stranger. I had a fear of embarrassment and always felt an overbearing sense of self-awareness that would lock me up inside. (I still struggle with this today.) But Josh wasn't like that. He seemed free from such restrictions. I liked Josh.

In the spring of my senior year I was on a school bus returning from an out-of-town tennis tournament. It was a sunny Saturday afternoon. I was hamming it up with my friends and we were all laughing and having a great time. We were even singing along to some Queen songs. Those were good times, good memories.

But the day turned dark and the notes went flat when we arrived back at the school. When we pulled up to the curb in front of the building, an administrator was standing there waiting for us. When the coach, who was driving the bus, stopped and opened the door, the administrator stepped on the bus and began whispering something into his ear. There was still some light chatter among the students on the bus, but it slowly faded as we all wanted to know what was going on. After a minute or two, the administrator stepped back while the coach stood to his feet. The coach turned to us, his face suddenly pale, and said, "Josh is dead."

The coach didn't know that Josh's girlfriend was on the bus. She was sitting catty-corner behind me. Everything is blurry in my memory from that point. It is as if someone placed frosted glass over the scenes in my mind—they play back fuzzy and in slow motion. Josh's girlfriend burst into tears, followed by screaming and convulsions. I felt dizzy and sick. I didn't know what to do so I did nothing. I hid, even on a bus filled with people. I sat still, quiet, and stared out the window, letting the scene around me fade to black.

Later that day I learned that Josh had committed suicide. His parents had gone out that morning to the grocery store, and while they were gone he shot himself in the head with a .22 caliber gun. No one saw it coming. If you had asked every parent, teacher, and student who knew Josh if they considered him a risk for suicide, they would have all chuckled and shook their heads, thinking the question was ridiculous. Josh seemed to represent life and joy. But now Josh was gone and no one was laughing.

I felt numb in the days following Josh's death, like nothing made sense to me. I was angry, confused, queasy, and disconnected. My insides were boiling and churning, but I shared these feelings with no one. I stuffed them into the ever-increasing storage house of secrets deep within my soul. I didn't know how to handle them, so I ignored them and stored them away, thinking they might decay and disappear over time. But secrets never disappear by ignoring them. In fact, they only seem to grow in the dark.

Josh's funeral was emotionally traumatizing for me. Someone made the outrageous decision to hold an open-casket funeral. That was a poor decision. Since Josh had shot himself in the head, there was major reconstructive work done on his face. It didn't even look like Josh. It didn't even look like a decent mannequin of Josh. I felt like I was going to vomit when I walked by the casket. That disfigured image of Josh remains with me to this day, and is not a memory I like having. These too were thoughts and feelings I stuffed. I walked out of that funeral home, dragging my secret feelings of grief, pain, and terrible confusion, making sure no one could tell the chains I bore.

******

This, unfortunately, was not my first encounter with death. Just two years prior to Josh's funeral I endured two other tragedies, one involving my cousin and the other my grandfather. By the time Josh's funeral occurred, I was growing weary of death. A "numbness" was spreading inside me. My heart felt heavy, burdened with sorrows I could not carry, but I had no choice.

My cousin, Craig, who was five years older than I, contracted HIV in 1990. This raised all kinds of questions in my mind concerning homosexuality, premarital sex, and more. With my own growing list of sexual secrets, I silently wondered if I might face a similar fate, but I spent very little time considering such thoughts.

Craig quickly fell ill with AIDS and died shortly thereafter. I was deeply grieved when he died but felt completely inadequate to express my sorrow. Craig was another person who always represented life, fun, and enthusiasm to me. His smile would widen across his entire face, and when he had an idea for an "adventure" there most certainly was a devilish sparkle in his eyes. Like the adventure that nearly killed me.

When I was eight years old, my family lived in Maryland. One spring, Craig and Keith (his younger brother) came to visit. Behind our house were miles of biking trails that crawled in all directions through the woods. One of these trails wound down a steep, long hill. We had a small, red metal wagon that could fit two kids in it at a time. Craig got the brilliant idea that Keith and I should ride in the wagon down this steep hill, which had a rather sharp turn at the bottom. Since I was younger than both Craig and Keith I didn't really have a vote. So, Keith and I hopped in the wagon and Craig began to push us down the hill. But I saw the sparkle flash in Craig's eyes and I knew something was about to happen I was not ready for. And it did.

At first, Craig just got the wagon rolling with a gentle push, but within a few strides he dropped his shoulder and launched us like a land-roving rocket down that hill. I heard the wheels squeaking and rattling, trying not to pop off their hot-spinning axles. The faster we flew down the hill, the more the wagon started to shake and bounce as it hit small rocks and twigs on the asphalt trail. Faster and faster I saw the bottom of the hill approaching and it dawned on me that we had no way to stop the wagon, or turn it when we reached the oncoming bend in the path.

We finally reached the bottom of the hill and Keith tried to turn the wagon by rapidly shifting his weight to one side. That didn't work. As soon as the wagon tilted, we began what I was sure to be a death roll. Arms and legs were flying, I was seeing sky, grass, wagon wheels, and I'm pretty certain a few tweety birds were hovering around my head as well. When the dust finally settled, I lifted my head, tears forming in my eyes, and saw Craig and Keith laughing with glee at the "adventure" we just had. I'm also convinced that Craig, without a scratch on him, winked at me.

These are my memories of Craig. He was fun, crazy, and full of life in the moment. He may have also been conflicted, but he still brought much joy to many people. I miss Craig. I miss the laugh, the smile, his unique sense of humor. I even miss how he could get offended at a family function and throw glances that meant something, and not something nice.

When Craig died, I remembered these times we shared together and felt a warmth and admiration for him. But I didn't know how to express these emotions to his parents, or to anyone, at his funeral. I learned, instead, to "grieve" as I saw others grieve. Try to cry when others were crying, be quiet when no one was talking, stare at the floor when others looked away. I didn't know how to say "I hurt too" or "I sure could go for one more push down the hill."

******

Shortly after Craig died, my dad's father, Paw Paw, died of a heart attack. It wasn't his first heart attack, but it was the one that eventually got him. Paw Paw was easily the toughest man I knew. Shaking his hand as a kid I felt like I was touching a brick. His hands were calloused and thick from years of manual labor. For many of those years he was a truck driver, hauling all sorts of different cargo. I wish I had spent more time with him, listening to his stories.

I remember one story he told of getting stung all over his head by a swarm of bees. As he was telling the story, my eyes were widening in amazement and anticipation. Then, with as much drama as he could muster, he told me (almost as an aside) that he was allergic to bee stings. His head swelled up the size of a watermelon and he barely survived the attack. He smiled and let out a soft chuckle, his eyes glancing away as he remembered the story. I could only stare in awe at this hulk of a man who cheated death, my Paw Paw. I wish I spent more time with him.

Although Paw Paw didn't talk much, when he did it was either very funny or very wise. His sense of humor was dry and often came with the sly sparkle in his eye that must have been passed down to Craig, because they were both characters.

As with Craig's death, when Paw Paw died I ignored and stuffed away the deep emotions I felt. I didn't know how to express affection in life, so how could I possibly express grief in death? But I still felt the pain. I felt the loss. And all these feelings were neatly placed in the dark closet of my heart, along with my shame, self-consciousness, and private fantasies. Slowly but steadily darkness was taking me over. I didn't recognize it at the time, but my paradigm of keeping secrets was pushing me ever further away from life and dangerously closer to death and despair. But my death wouldn't be like Josh's, Craig's, or Paw Paw's. Mine would be a death of the heart, a death of the soul.

******

Pile upon pile, the secrets mounted. They weren't all sexual secrets, but they produced the same result: loneliness and isolation. The path of least resistance, which I was becoming accustomed to travel, was leading me to a chamber of horrible death. And I didn't even know it.

Living in the Light

Death is part of life, but not always a part we like talking about. So we hide our feelings about the topic. We might be afraid of death, confused about death, or just ignorant of it. Regardless, we must all face it, our own death as well as the death of those we love. You cannot escape death. (How's that for a "feel good" moment?)

Have you lost someone you loved? How did you respond? Did you stuff your emotions, hiding the pain, the anger, the fear, the confusion? If you did, you aren't alone. I can relate to those reactions. But I want to invite you to now chart a new course, to face death and grief with a new resolve. Face the darkness of death in the light of love.

You will not reduce the pain of death by loving less—or more. So, let me challenge you to love more. Death hurts, but love those in your life today as if there will be no tomorrow. If you do, you will one day face their passing with no more regrets.

High & Low

Experiencing the death of a loved one changes you. I can't really explain how it changes you, but it does. It seems like it lifts a curtain on the characters of life around you, and you get a brief glimpse of something beyond this world, beyond the façade of so-called life. You can't quite grasp what lies behind the curtain, but if you have ever witnessed another person die, you know something is there. I faced this encounter with the Beyond the summer after I graduated high school. The person I saw die was my father.

******

I mentioned earlier that I was an all-star basketball player in high school. Being somewhat of a late bloomer, I wasn't noticed by many of the larger colleges, but was still somehow selected to the Texas McDonald's Basketball All-Star Game. It was quite a thrill to open that invitation and see my name as one of the players invited. I received the invitation during the spring semester of my senior year, even though the game would not be played until July. This gave me some time to get the word out and also get prepared for such an incredible experience.

The All-Star game was a big deal. All the athletes were housed in the dorms at SMU in Fort Worth and received top notch, all-star treatment for an entire week. We ate our meals together, interviewed with local newspapers and TV stations, and practiced daily for the upcoming game on Saturday. It was a rush! I felt important, even a bit famous (despite the fact that nobody outside the gym would have known my name). I must admit I liked the feeling of being "somebody" and getting noticed for accomplishing something very few others could do.

My basking in the sunlight of my own greatness (ha-ha) came to an end halfway through the all-star week. I was informed that I had a phone call. I trotted down the hallway to the phone in my dorm room. I picked up the receiver, "Hello."

"Hi, Jonathan, it's me," said my mother. "Your dad is in the hospital."

I know my mother said other things after that, but most of it sounded like white noise on a TV set to me. "Your dad is in the hospital." The phrase kept repeating in my head, rattling around like a loose marble in a tin cup. How could this be? How could the strongest man I know be in a place for the weak and the ill?

I couldn't process the magnitude of such a situation. So, I went into management mode, ensuring that my mother knew I was "OK" and that it wouldn't affect me having a good time at the all-star camp. I hung up the phone, wandered aimlessly down the hallway toward the gym, and jumped back into practice as if nothing was wrong. But everything was wrong.

I believe everyone reacts to bad news differently. Some react with grand outward expressions of grief or anger or fear. Others might react with perplexity and befuddlement. At the time I received the news of my dad being in the hospital I had already developed a substantial history of reacting to any negative news by withdrawing and isolating. I might have been physically present on the phone with my mom, but my mind and emotions were hurdling at light speed away from the reality that bad news had just landed in my lap. Escapism was my favored path to travel and I had spent years becoming very familiar with its route.

I suppose you might like to know what landed my dad in the hospital. The simple answer: a big heart.

Almost a year prior, Daddy had a routine physical that detected his heart was enlarged and wasn't pumping at optimum efficiency. At that time all the doctor could prescribe was an adjusted diet that reduced his salt and sugar intake. They didn't know the cause of the enlargement or of any medicinal treatment to combat it. In fact, the doctor was perplexed at how fit and active Daddy was with such a weakening heart. But that was just because the doctor didn't really know my dad.

Daddy did very little to change his activity patterns over the following year, although he did manage to improve his diet some. But there wasn't a lot he could improve upon because he was a relatively healthy eater, aside from his daily dose of Oreo cookies. In my mind, though, he more than compensated for a few cookies through his relentless hard, physical work.

Every weekend Daddy would work on our property; trimming trees, hauling and burning brush, and dozens of other physically demanding chores. I privately idolized my dad, amazed at his physical strength and stamina. I knew he wasn't a terribly young man (he was 37 when I was born, early-50's by my high school years), but his work ethic was incredible, like that of someone half his age. He represented everything consistent with real manhood: hard work, integrity, and perseverance.

So, when I heard that Daddy (a man among boys in my mind) was in the hospital, my world froze. I never could have imagined a weakness in him, at least not physically. And even the weaknesses I did witness, he pushed through those with toughness and resolve. Like the times he used to play catch with me.

Daddy had arthritis in his right shoulder. He never mentioned it much, and with the activities he engaged in you wouldn't have known it bothered him. When I first got involved in sports in junior high, I was the quarterback of the football team. I remember going out in the backyard, fully dressed in my football gear, and tossing the pigskin with Daddy. I would cock my arm and zing a spiral right into his chest. Sometimes Daddy would catch it, sometimes not. But when he would wind up to throw the ball back to me, I would notice him grit his teeth and even let out a muffled wince. He was in pain. But he never said a word. He never asked to quit or do something else. His love for me was greater than his own pain. I will never forget his sacrifice, his example of fatherly love in those backyard moments. Even though I didn't know how to express my feelings to him (or anyone else) at the time, I loved him. I always loved him.

Why is it so hard sometimes to verbalize affection to those you love the most? This has baffled me all my life. I loved my dad, I truly did. But I always felt awkward and disjointed in my attempts to express my love for him. I felt a discomfort, my eyes would dart and words never came to mind, and my thoughts became consumed with how to flee the conversation as soon as possible.

Ironically, in my private moments, I could elegantly and thoroughly capture my feelings and express them in imaginary conversations in my head. I could look Daddy straight in the eye, use meaningful words, and even embrace him. But I couldn't do such things in the real world, when he was standing right in front of me day after day. I know he felt the same way, because I witnessed him fumble all over his words and struggle with how to show a teenage boy physical affection, so the difficulty was a two-way street. But I still wonder why these barriers exist where there is no logical reason for them to be.

Because of my love for Daddy (albeit buried love) I had very mixed emotions about my time at the all-star game. My mind was divided between wanting to soak up all the fun and excitement of the game, while also wondering what they were doing to my dad in the hospital. I was experiencing that old, familiar feeling of highs and lows occurring simultaneously (remember my tree stump experience?). But by now my emotions were growing tired, confused, and unsure how to respond to the darker realities of life. As always, I stuffed my deepest feelings in an attempt to appear strong rather than weak. Just more secrets to smother my already drowning heart.

******

In spite of the negative circumstances, the All-Star game really was fun. I scored thirteen points and had a great time hooping it up with the best players in Texas. My mother, sister, a whole bunch of my extended family, and some close friends attended the game. Daddy even got to listen to the game on the radio in his hospital room (kind of like Shooter did in one of my favorite movies, *Hoosiers*). But when the game was over and the "high" of the all-star week wore off, I began to crumble—privately, of course. Every high in life is followed by a low, which is followed by a high, and so on. Life is seasonal and cyclical. My lows, however, seemed to be mounting and I didn't know how to proceed through them to the anticipated high on the other end. I felt like I just kept tumbling down the stairsteps of emotion, one low at a time. I feared hitting bottom, if there even was a bottom, and what that would look like. At the time, it looked like not having a dad.

Living in the Light

Have you hidden your true feelings for the ones you love the most? Why is it so hard for us to express our deepest emotions to our spouse, our friends, or our family? Maybe you don't struggle with this, but if you do, you know what I am talking about. We hide our true feelings behind our secure walls of perfectionism, pride, and fear.

What conflicting emotions do you struggle with in your life? Happiness and sadness, fear and faith, anger and peace? Are you prone to expressing only the "positive" emotions without regard to their counterpart? Let me encourage you not to ignore the uncomfortable, "negative" emotions. They are valid and need to be expressed as well, in healthy, constructive ways.

Bring your conflicted emotions out into the light with those you love. It may feel unpleasant and scary at first, but over time the bond you create in your relationships will form a safety your heart has always longed for.

Frustrated Manhood

Every boy who graduates high school and ventures off to college (or whatever else) feels like he is transitioning from boyhood to manhood. The problem is that no boy knows how to be a man. It is not hardwired into him. Manhood is learned. Boys must be taught how to become men. Those who have no one to teach them end up pretending to be a man. But the act doesn't fool anyone, at least not for long.

I entered college in the fall of 1992, with a future full of uncertainty and anxiety (can I hear an "Amen!"). College was a new experience. Living on my own was also new territory. And launching into adulthood with my dad in the hospital didn't help my confidence. But life went on. The sun rose every morning, my heart kept beating, and I played my part as best I could. I didn't know what I was doing, in college, in family, or in life. But I could pretend very well.

Before you conclude that my entire life up to this point was fraudulent, let me assure you it wasn't. Like I said in the previous chapter, life is seasonal and cyclical. I had many positive moments of spiritual insight and growth, along with genuinely precious moments with friends and family during my adolescence. I don't discount the importance of those moments simply because I was simultaneously weaving a thread of secrecy and dividedness into my being. We all become the sum of our histories, the good and the bad. The months my dad was in the hospital were actually a good season for me spiritually, despite my pretending to be strong when I felt very, very weak.

******

Daddy was sitting up in his bed when I walked in to visit him after the all-star week was over. It was a bit surreal to see him in his hospital gown, surrounded by all the pumps and monitors that accompany all hospital rooms. My dad had worked as a nurse for over thirty years, so I wasn't unfamiliar with hospitals, but it felt as if things were out of place to see him in the bed instead of leaning over it to help a patient.

I smiled and said hi and we talked about what the doctors were saying and how he was feeling and all that normal small talk stuff. He said he felt fine and that the doctors were saying the only long-term solution to his condition was a heart transplant. This was another hard blow for me to take. I knew there had been incredible advances in transplant procedures over the decades, but I also knew this was no small surgery and the recovery could be brutal. I wondered what the waiting procedure was like and what was necessary to "qualify" for an available heart.

August was a long, busy month. I was preparing to go away to college and visiting Daddy as much as possible in the hospital, which was a two-hour drive one way (the best facility for his particular illness was in Dallas, north of the small town in central Texas where we lived). Several trips I had friends go with me, but a number of my drives to the hospital I traveled alone. Many times on those trips I would think about Daddy and his need for a new, strong heart. I loved him so much. I sometimes daydreamed about calling 911 to report an accident just before driving my car off the road into a telephone pole so I could give Daddy my own heart. Thankfully, reasonable thinking would always prevail as I worked through the irrationality of such thoughts.

I felt like I was actually growing spiritually during that season of my life. I was reading my Bible and praying. I was praying a lot, mostly asking questions. Questions like, "Why does God allow good, honorable people to suffer?"

"What was God's purpose for letting Daddy get sick?"

"What was I supposed to do?"

"Could I do anything to help or must I just be an observer?"

Even though I felt lost, confused by all the questions that didn't seem to have any answers, I also felt God's presence. I knew he cared, even though I didn't think he was expressing his care very well at the time. Above all, I knew God was real, as evidenced by Daddy's faith through his whole sickness.

I remember visiting Daddy one day and hearing him say he was in a "win-win" situation. That statement got my attention because it didn't seem win-win to me. He explained that if he were to receive a heart transplant he would have additional time with us, his family, and that would bring great joy to his life. But he went on to share that if God should take him home, his joy would be indescribable. In his eyes, it was win-win.

Seeing my dad experience joy while growing weaker and weaker, being daily probed and pricked, was a memory that solidified to me the realness of God as One who walks with us to the very end. Only God could produce that kind of joy in a dying man.

My mom also demonstrated great faith during those months. She clung to the following verses of Scripture during Daddy's time in the hospital.

******

Though the fig tree does not bud and there are no grapes on the vines, though the olive crop fails and the fields produce no food, though there are no sheep in the pen and no cattle in the stalls, yet I will rejoice in the LORD, I will be joyful in God my Savior. (Habakkuk 3:17–18)

I didn't fully comprehend how one could rejoice and be joyful when the chips were down, but regardless, I was seeing real-life faith displayed through my parents. These memories would eventually prove priceless in the coming years when my life completely fell apart and all that remained were barren fig trees, fruitless vines, and empty stalls (metaphorically speaking).

******

At the end of August 1992 I entered college. I immediately enjoyed the atmosphere, meeting new people, and the energy that came from a new adventure. My personality has always been drawn to trying new things, so college was a good transition for me. But because of the newness of it all I didn't have any close friends (not that I had any prior to this time either). I didn't have anyone to share my fears concerning my dad's condition. And when I did tell anyone about him being in the hospital, I would readily play the part of a guy who had it all together or didn't seem to need any help. I didn't know how to gauge who was safe to be vulnerable with, so I simply remained distant and disconnected. Daddy's condition worsened rapidly. The process of receiving a heart transplant is not simple. There is a waiting list, and your place on the list is not simply first-come-first-served. Multiple factors have to line up. First, there is a ranking by date admitted. Then, there have to be blood type matches, tissue matches, and other factors that I can't even remember. Finally, the receptor (my dad) has to be strong enough to endure the surgery. As Daddy grew weaker and weaker, other organs had to pick up the slack to make up for his failing heart. Because of this, his lungs were working extremely hard to deliver oxygen, and were therefore being overtaxed. The situation, by the middle of September, looked bleak. I received another phone call from my mom asking me to come to the hospital. She felt the end was coming soon for Daddy.

September 23, 1992 is a day I will never forget. Daddy had lost nearly one hundred pounds in two months. His skin hung on his bones. He could not move his arms or legs on his own, and his cheeks sunk deep into his face, exposing the shape of his skull beneath. On that day he was incoherent, unable to focus his eyes, move his head, or respond to anyone. I remember the fear I felt sitting next to his bed, never having witnessed someone pass from here to the Beyond. I didn't know what to expect, and I certainly had no idea how I would react.

That morning the doctors had a meeting with my mom. They told her she had two options. One, they could keep Daddy alive on various machines, but the probability of him regaining enough strength for any operation, let alone a heart transplant, was negligible. Two, the doctors could pull the plugs on Daddy's machines and ensure his physical comfort by increasing his morphine drip, but this would mean death was a certainty, whether it be a few minutes or several days.

Looking back, I can't imagine being in my mom's position on that day. No wife ever wants to have to make such a heart-wrenching decision. But my mom, again displaying strength of faith and resolve, opted for Daddy's comfort. She truly exhibited the character of a real helpmate, desiring to do only the best for the man she loved for twenty-three years. At my mom's request, the doctors pulled the plug.

The final moments of Daddy's life impacted me profoundly, and sometimes still do. My sister and my mom were sitting by his bed, opposite from me. They were talking to Daddy, saying goodbye, telling him they would be OK and that they loved him. I sat silent, holding his hand, trying to compose myself and deal with the frightening nature of the coming moment of death. I kept looking at Daddy's face, looking for any sign of him understanding what was going on, wanting to know if he was hearing anything, or seeing anything. My mom started repeating that is was OK for Daddy to go.

I again stared at his face. Nothing, no expression.

I knew the time was now or never if I was going to share any last words with the man who meant everything to me. I leaned over the bed and whispered into his right ear, "Daddy, it's OK. I love you. You can go now." At that moment, Daddy squeezed my hand. Less than five minutes later, he was gone.

I believe God has a way of marking memories in our lives because of their importance, and then providing guideposts along the way so we can find our way back to them. This precious exchange in the final moments of my dad's life was such a memory. It was as if my dad was waiting to hear that his son was OK, willing to step into the next phase of the journey to manhood. When Daddy squeezed my hand, I felt his blessing, his affirmation being passed on, commissioning me to bear the mantle of manhood he had carried so faithfully. I only wish that I had taken that commission more seriously at the time.

As soon as Daddy's heart monitor flatlined, I lost it. By that time, our pastor had entered the room. I stood up, turned toward him, and sobbed into his chest. My body convulsed as I couldn't veil the eruption of buried, intense feelings.

Interestingly, even as I wrote these last few paragraphs, the intensity of that emotion overwhelmed me and I sobbed again, not because I haven't grieved the loss but rather because of the magnitude of that memory and for the fact that I didn't take advantage of what it meant at the time: an opportunity to begin a new journey and live with no regrets.

Living in the Light

Fathers have a profound impact on their children. God designed it this way. For some, this impact was amazingly positive and brings back many cherished memories. For others, this impact was terribly negative and has left painful scars and tormenting memories. Either way, our dads weren't perfect. But somewhere inside each of us there has always been a deep desire to love him.

Have you ever wondered why the desire a child has to please his father is so strong? I believe it stems from a deeper desire our heavenly Father has placed in us to connect with him. He loves us more than our earthly fathers ever could, and he wants us to experience that love right here, right now. But first, you have to deal with your daddy's false image. The first image of God you ever had was your dad. Because of this, you had a skewed image, an imperfect understanding of who God really is. So, in order to embrace God's love in its fullness, its perfect, untarnished state, you must seek to heal from the imperfect image created through your dad. This may require forgiving him for things he did that were insensitive or abusive. It might mean acknowledging that your dad wasn't perfect, that he hid his flaws and deceived you about who he really was.

God wants to heal your hurts connected to your dad. And God is the only one who can—he made it that way.

Fuel

I didn't deal well with Daddy dying. I suppose few, if any, handle the death of a parent well. I didn't know how to grieve and I was too proud to tell anyone (remember, secrets). So instead I just got angry, really angry. I primarily directed my anger at God and it got brutal; ugly, actually.

Just as everyone reacts differently to bad news, everyone also expresses anger differently. I wasn't a big public displayer of my anger. I boiled on the inside and would let the lava of my anger seep out from the edges of my life. Some might have called this a sort of "passive aggressive" expression of anger. Call it whatever you want, it wasn't pretty. And "letting it all out" didn't do any good in helping me get past the fact that my dad was gone. I felt completely lost in the choppy sea of manhood without a compass.

I remember one night, about a week after my dad died, I was on my college campus at the Baptist Student Union where I had made a few friends and was becoming increasingly involved with the student ministries there. I think there was a Bible study going on or something, but I just couldn't hang around. I was too distracted with a million other thoughts going through my head. I got up, went outside, and sat underneath a row of bushes that separated two buildings. Then, I let God have it.

I can't recall how long I was under those bushes, but I remember there wasn't anybody left on campus by the time I walked back to my dorm room. I told God what I thought of him, that I didn't believe he was kind or compassionate, and that he must not care about me much to take the one man who I believed could lead me into manhood.

I cried. I kicked bushes. I beat my fists on the ground, on my chest, and I am sure I would have knocked out anybody who might have tried to crawl under there and "help" me. The bottom line was that I was steamed and felt powerless against the overwhelming flow of emotions.

When I have shared this part of my story with some people they have responded, "It's good to express your anger, especially getting it out to God." While that may be true, there was one fundamental flaw in why I expressed my anger that night: I didn't want it resolved. I didn't flare up at God because I wanted comfort or resolution or change. No, I sent zingers toward God because I wanted to vent. Period. And because that was my only reason for spouting off, I didn't feel any better on my walk home later that night. I went to bed angry and woke up the next day in no better condition. I was using my anger to push God away, not to seek his comfort or guidance.

******

Secrets are like gasoline to sexually addictive behaviors. But secret anger is the oxygen. I didn't know that you have to deal with anger if you are going to get clean from sex addiction. Not that I cared about getting clean during college since I didn't even admit I had a sexual addiction. But my addictive behaviors, and pattern of disconnection, began to manifest themselves in different avenues. One such avenue was dating.

Through my involvement in the BSU (Baptist Student Union, later the Baptist Student Center), I met several girls that caught my fancy. I began dating one girl soon after my dad's funeral. She was sympathetic and caring, knowing firsthand what it was like to lose a loved one unexpectedly. There seemed to be genuine care between us, but ultimately I pulled back from the relationship due to my secrets and a growing (albeit undetected) fear of intimacy. We dated for maybe three months. When the relationship needed to go deeper, I froze. I didn't know how to deal with any relationship that went beyond mere friendship because I didn't know how to share authentically the things that resided deeper in my soul. Those seemed like dark places to me, places that even I didn't venture to explore, let alone let someone else poke around. I didn't know how to navigate those areas in a way that didn't feel like I was threatening my very existence. I perceived that this girl might want to go deeper, might even want to explore the "inner me." So, I broke up with her.

Of course, I did the whole "It's not you, it's me" routine, but I don't think she bought it. Nevertheless, I was backpedaling as fast as I could to escape the possibility of having to share any of my secrets or to reveal the truth about my boiling anger and unresolved grief.

This eventually became my model for dating relationships in college. Meet, flirt, befriend, date, freak out, dump. Several more times I would repeat this exact same model, never able to commit beyond several months of dating for fear of being exposed for the emotionally detached fraud I was. Through all these relationships the light of my heart was growing dimmer, as if it was drifting toward the horizon, and with each passing day it was shrinking and losing a little of its glow.

Shame was a big part of this dating pattern as well. I felt horrible when I would break up with these girls, I really did. But it was a weird combination of feeling sick for having broken a girl's heart, but elated that I was "free" again to explore new "territory." Looking back, it makes sense to see that my behaviors were also about control, not merely hiding secrets. This too is characteristic of addiction, always believing the delusion that control equals security. I now know that such thinking is total crap, but it sure explains a lot of what I was doing then. Control only ensured isolation and disconnectedness, and those were becoming hallmarks of my dating relationships.

******

Even while dating I was still looking at porn and mastur-bating. My fantasies expanded, though. I now had new girls to dream about, at work, at school, even at the BSU. Lust knows no boundaries when it comes to fantasy. These new friendships and acquaintances also provided additional fuel to the secret addiction I was building. And these fantasies were becoming an empty substitute for developing genuine, wholesome friendships with any of these girls, for they were becoming nothing more than mere pictures in my mind, pictures for my manipulation and pleasure. I was using them, not relating with them.

During my sophomore year in college, I began working full time managing a Chick-fil-A restaurant, and I loved the job. I loved the people I worked with even more. But some of my experiences with coworkers only increased my growing addic-tion. There were often after-work parties that involved alcohol, gambling, and other "late night" activities. I went right along with all of it, never taking a moral stand. More fuel to the fire.

My secret sexual addiction was growing, and nobody knew it but me. Porn, masturbation, fantasy, these were all increasing. More fuel from my surroundings at work and school were add-ing to the bonfire blazing within me. And nobody knew. But this is the nature of secrets, isn't it? The whole point of having a secret is so nobody knows the truth. And the only way anyone could have known my secret was for me to tell them. Therefore, the secret kept growing.

Living in the Light

Most people who develop a very sophisticated web of secrets become quite detached relationally. They feed their desire to escape, to disconnect, and to run from the pains of life, only to find that this leads to more pain. If you are going to live a truly abundant life, you must deal with the tendency to drift, to detach.

Do you regularly share your emotions with your spouse or trusted friends? Even the emotions that frighten and overwhelm you? Anger, especially, is a powerful emotion that naturally causes division and disconnection in relationships. But this doesn't mean it doesn't exist, or that it need not be talked about. We need to become skilled at "talking out" our anger with those we love, so our relationships do not divide any further.

Share what is on your heart with someone you love—today.

Conflictions

It is easy to hide behind Christianity, the religious "system" part anyway. I learned early on in life how to use my Christianity as a shield rather than the means for dealing with my growing insecurities and secret sins through a relationship with Jesus. My first two years in college would slowly crystallize this method of walling off the real me behind the facade of religious piety.

I became heavily involved in the BSU campus ministry. I plugged into a freshman Bible study class that met every week. I was at the BSU almost every time the doors were open. It was a place that was full of fun, safe people, just like church. I made friends quickly and found a group with whom I had a lot in common. Most everyone at the BSU had a long history of going to church, so they all understood the "system," although there were a few "radicals" who would challenge the norm from time to time (even daring to question such staples of righteousness as "no drinking" or "no dancing").

The friendships I was developing through the BSU were genuine. It wasn't as if I was consciously going up to a person with some kind of agenda to "fool" them into believing I was something I really wasn't. I truly liked these people, and they seemed to like me. And we would even talk about serious stuff, feelings we were having, trouble in various class subjects, and what our futures might look like. But underneath, deep down in the scary shadowy corners of my heart, there were clouds, dark places of confusion, doubts, and secrets. Because these places were so deep within me I wasn't always aware of what was going on down there. My daily interactions didn't require that I think much about the growing darkness in my soul, the "nighttime me" that was developing. Slowly, however, the night was enticing me and it would eventually overtake me.

Most of my freshman year in college I operated in the world of "daytime me," not spending much time acknowledging the growing nighttime me. This was where the fake Christianity came in, not in a conscious sort of way, but just by the nature of wanting to avoid dealing with the unsavory parts of my being. After all, you don't just blurt out in a group of college Christians, "I regularly fail managing my sexuality. I masturbate often, I lust all the time (even over some of you), I hate myself, and I wonder if God really cares." Such statements have the same effect on people as dropping a boulder in a pond has on water: retreat. So, I kept my mouth shut concerning such realities within me, and instead focused on trying to build friendships, fun friendships to compensate for my inner frustrations.

All my life I have made friends easily in whatever setting I am in. The same was true in college. I certainly had friends at the BSU, but I also had friends elsewhere. I had friends from the dorm, at work, in various academic departments, even among faculty. Part of the reason for having so many friends in so many places was that I liked being known. I suppose we all like to be known, to a degree.

By spreading myself around among all these acquaintances (and that's really all they were), I was, as they call it in financial circles, diversifying. It's like I was becoming a human relations mutual fund, not investing myself in one or two solid, deep friendships, but rather dividing myself up among many different people in many different settings. The overall effect of this "diversification" was that I built a very strong, impenetrable wall around those dark, shadowy places of my heart. Without even realizing it, I was preventing the one thing my heart longed for most: connection.

******

The summer between my freshman and sophomore year of college I went to Branson, Missouri to work at a Christian sports camp, Kanakuk. What a summer, an awkward summer. I was working at the camp as a counselor for eleven-year-old boys. The setting of the camp was beautiful, but it was a long way from home, a long way from what was familiar.

I enjoyed the camp setting, especially the times I had together with the staff. I realized, though, that I wasn't cut out for camp counseling because I didn't seem to enjoy my time with the kids as much as I did with the adults. I also learned that I didn't really have the personality for "camp life." You need to be a little crazy, bold, and even a bit danger-seeking. I, however, am not like that. I have always been more of a verbal person, choosing to engage in the volleying of words, not wanting to see who can catapult themselves highest into the air off "The Blob." These were valuable insights into me, what made me tick, and hopefully my learning curve didn't cause any of the campers who were under my care to hate their time at camp that summer.

I also felt like I was growing spiritually that summer, at least a little. Being so far away from home, I felt more compelled to read my Bible and pray for my own sake, not necessarily because it was expected (even though it was expected, being a counselor and all).

But also being far from home gave me the undeniable feeling of being anonymous, unknown among my peers. We would have short stints of time off over the weekends, mainly for doing laundry and other personal chores. Every time the campers would leave and it became "my time," I would feel the urge to want to get by myself, to disconnect. It is a feeling that is a little hard to explain.

I guess I could explain the feeling as an issue of control. I like to be in control (don't we all?). Working at camp during the week, I was not in control. The camp schedule controlled me. There were times and places for everything. Breakfast, same time every morning. Activities, lunch, cabin cleanup, sports, dinner, and on and on. No personal time. No control. So, as soon as the campers were gone, control, or at least the perception of control, returned. And when control returned, my first inclination was to get alone and do whatever I felt like doing.

Most of the time, when I got alone I didn't do anything inappropriate *per se*. This was largely due to the fact that I didn't know the area very well, and the few friends I had at the camp I had only known for a couple of weeks. I would drive around the town, stopping in here and there to check out various shops or theatres. I had no plan, but it didn't matter. I had control, and that felt more important than having a plan.

During those months in Branson I felt my dividedness grow. I was developing a fondness for one of the female counselors. What I thought was real affection, real sparks, she confirmed was only boyhood hormones. I can't say I was crushed when she refused my affection, but it did cause me to stumble backward some. I was sure she felt the same way about me that I did for her.

When she told me it couldn't work (we lived in different states), I stuffed my true feelings into the corner and simply responded as if it was no skin off my nose. The truth was that I didn't like it when I was wrong, when I misread a person. And I didn't like taking the risk of being vulnerable and then not having things go my way. But somewhere along my history I learned to disengage and not talk about those feelings. It felt safer to hide discomfort and disappointment than to deal with it out in the open.

I finished out my time at Kanakuk feeling kind of numb, and a little more divided. A few more important, strong feelings got locked away where nobody could see them, and the conflict in my soul only increased.

******

The beginning of my sophomore year in college I took over the leadership responsibilities of the freshman Bible study at the BSU. I was now teaching the class, and I was having fun. I liked teaching (still do). I liked bringing fresh ideas to a bunch of empty-headed freshman looking to me for answers. OK, it wasn't that bad, but that's how the upperclassmen perceived most freshmen. Regardless, it was a forum where I could be heard and also hear the ideas of others, and I liked that atmosphere.

Without realizing what was happening, however, I began using my position of a teacher as a shield to prevent people from getting too close. I learned, almost on a subconscious level, that if I was perceived as someone with answers (i.e. Teacher) then people were less prone to ask probing, personal questions of me. Most interactions remained subject-related rather than person-related. Questions centered on finding some static answer to a problem with a certain subject, rather than personal questions intended to find out more about who I was. I easily gravitated to these types of positions and through them I naturally built up secure walls around my heart, which only reinforced the existing walls. (This principle can explain why so many pastors and church leaders fall to sexual sin: there is no accountability for those who "have all the answers.")

I didn't recognize it at the time, but these "spiritual leadership" positions actually helped "nighttime Jonathan" grow stronger. By building a sort of emotional cocoon, impenetrable by even those closest to me, it became easier and easier for me to slip into the darkness of my growing addiction to self, lust, and pornography. Ironically, the religious world that I had assumed would pull me out of the trap I was in was instead silently aiding in pushing me closer and closer to the noose that would eventually suffocate me. I wanted something that world could offer, but not in the way they seemed to be offering it, as a set of rules and rigid preferences. I understand now that what I wanted was a real connection with Jesus. But few in the religious world seemed to know where I could find him.

Living in the Light

Have you spread yourself thin when it comes to your relationships? Do you have one or two truly deep, intimate friendships? If your only "deep" friend is your spouse, you need to stretch yourself a bit. I think we all need a small handful of people who know us inside and out, truly everything about who we really are.

How are you dealing with the issue of control in your life? Are you OK with life not always going your way or all your desires being met? How are you processing these moments (or seasons) of disappointment? These are the times in life where you need people who know you, who listen to you, who support you, and who challenge you. If your habit has been to simply stuff these disappointments and attempt to tighten the reigns of control in your life, you are not making progress toward living in the light. Loosen your grip, listen to wise counsel, and let God lead.

Oh, also, one other side note. Regularly encourage your pastor to pursue and deepen these same types of friendships. Don't be party to him becoming isolated and picked off as another victim of sexual temptation. Just a helpful idea for keeping your church healthy from the top down.

The Light

Tension. This is what occurs in a life of secrets, a life of dividedness. The greater the divide became in my life between what was "in the light" and what was "in the dark," the greater tension I felt. Tension is like filling a ball with air beyond its proper capacity. If you continue pumping air into the ball, without any way to release the pressure, eventually the ball bursts. This is how secrecy operated in my life. My disconnectedness and isolation pumped foul air into the balloon of my soul.

Because I didn't like this tension (nobody does) I wanted an answer, something to relieve this growing pressure. I tried a lot of things. I prayed, but never felt anyone was listening (at least not long enough to keep me from eventually going back to the dark). I tried willpower, "promising" to never again do any of the dark deeds that were gradually becoming part of my life's routine. Busyness was another outlet, reasoning that if I could just distract myself with enough activity I could prevent myself from engaging in the secretive sexual outlets of porn, fantasy, and masturbation. But all my efforts to relieve the tension only led to frustration and failure. And the tension simply expanded.

During my first two years of college I went through a handful of short-term girlfriends, always trying to play a part I felt inadequate to play. Whenever I would date someone I felt like such a fraud, this phony guy pretending to be Mr. Wonderful, while secretly I knew I wasn't measuring up to whatever expectations they had of me. I could play the role of "nice guy" very well, and it always got my foot in the door of beginning relationships. But it usually didn't take long before a dating relationship would hit certain key points in which it either had to go deeper or end. They all ended. I couldn't go deeper. I wouldn't go deeper. Part of me was afraid of exposing myself as a phony, but another part became tired of the "game" of dating, the seeming exclusivity that grew with each date.

I realize I am sounding like the stereotypical jerk who gets the girl on phony charm, grows weary of the mounting responsibilities and perceived pressures of a budding relationship, and flings her to the side in pursuit of the next one. While I wasn't this blatant, or even aware of such a likely perception by onlookers, this is in a sense what was happening. I was being a self-centered jerk when it came to my dating relationships. I was only looking out for my interests, making sure my secret stayed securely protected, unthreatened by a mere girlfriend. This cycle repeated itself several times in those first two years of college. The summer between my sophomore and junior year would prove to be a significant test of my character. A test I failed miserably.

******

I was working an afternoon shift, not really paying much attention to what I was doing, when I caught a glimpse of a new hire in the back of the store. I couldn't see her face but other employees were talking to her like she had worked there the previous summer. She appeared attractive, at least from the view I had of the back of her head. I started looking for excuses to go to the back room just so I could get a better look at her. Finally, one of our boxes of fries was empty, so I had my chance.

I quickly snatched the empty box and headed to the freezer in the back to replace it with a full one. As I rounded the corner, she turned to see who was coming. Our eyes met and we both smiled that silly, gawky smile that makes it immediately transparent to everyone witnessing the smile that mutual attraction has struck. I completed my shift, but not without first finding out her name and taking a peek at what her schedule was going to be in the coming days.

Jess (not her real name) quickly became my focal point of the summer of '94. We hit it off great at work and had an easy time making conversation. There was certainly an instant attraction between us, more than just friends. We flirted, smiled, giggled, acted all the stupid ways that people act when falling in love. I had no idea where things would lead, but I didn't think much about it. I was having fun and Jess made me feel good.

One night Jess and I went to a parking lot to talk and look at the stars. We sat out on the trunk of the car and talked and talked. As we grew more and more comfortable with each other, the point finally came where we were facing each other, wondering what to do next. You know, that awkward, yet unmistakable moment, when you know a kiss is the next thing on the agenda, but there is still the little bit of confusion of how to cross that bridge gracefully. So, I simply asked Jess if I could kiss her. Not the most romantic line, but effective. The rest of that night there wasn't much more talking.

Our relationship shifted quickly after the kiss. I felt things hit warp speed in a matter of weeks. Our physical relationship escalated and I found myself looking forward to our time together more for what I could enjoy physically than necessarily anything we could talk about or "connect" on emotionally. This relationship was feeding parts of my secret addiction and I fell headlong into it without even slowing down to consider what might happen next.

Sex is a powerful thing. I believe God made it that way on purpose. Sex is supposed to be a key component to melding two

lives together permanently. But just like fire, if it is used outside
safe boundaries, it destroys. I was learning this lesson the hard
way, by repeatedly being burned by the fires of sexual experience outside the boundary of marriage. My relationship with
Jess might have burned me the worst.

Over the summer, it became apparent that Jess and I weren't
going to make it as a couple. Our lives were going in different
directions, we were attending school in different states, and heat
from our physical intimacy was the only thing that seemed to be
holding us together. Eventually, we broke up. She was upset. I
was upset. I was also angry, very angry. Not at Jess. I was angry
with myself. I once again went down the pathway of selfishness
and lust and, not surprisingly, found the same thing that I found
all the other times I traveled its path: loneliness and shame.

Life has a way of working in cycles. Night turns into day as
the earth revolves around the sun. Fruit that falls to the ground
and dies plants seeds that will eventually grow more fruit. When
one chapter of life closes, losing a job, the death of a loved one,
or ending a friendship, another one opens. A sad, lonely chapter
was ending in my life that summer. But a new, fresh chapter was
just around the corner, I just couldn't see it yet.

******

I clearly remember the moment I met my future wife. It was
a hot August day in 1994. I was just starting my junior year in
college and she was a freshman. I had decided to go to a campus
ministries progressive dinner (each ministry served a different
course of the meal) to "check out" the incoming students for
that semester. I had no idea what I was in for that night.

I filled my plate, then turned to find a seat. The room was
packed with college students gearing up for the coming months
of study and fun. I walked toward a table, and stopped short
when I saw her. She was smiling, laughing at something someone

at the table just said. Her captivating brown eyes caught me off guard. They danced as she laughed. I quickly grabbed a seat across from her and her friend. I introduced myself, and thus began "the rest of my life," a new chapter that sparked hope.

I remember the feeling I had when I met Elaine. It was a feeling of freshness, of sensing purity and authenticity. It came through her eyes. You can tell a lot about a person through their eyes.

Up to that point in my life I had known very few people who didn't have something hidden behind their eyes. Like a veil, their eyes would cover their secrets, darting and averting to prevent the darkness from being seen. But Elaine's eyes didn't cover anything. The first time I saw her and looked into her eyes, I knew I was seeing her, the real, unhidden person. This mesmerized me and instantly captivated my attention. Her purity of heart drew me to her.

We continued together through all the stops of the progressive dinner, asking lots of "get to know you" questions. She was direct with her answers, kind in her tone, seemingly genuinely interested in what I had to say. We finished the dinner, said our goodbyes, and went our separate ways. I went home that night feeling good, like I had experienced something wholesome and right. It's as if a ray of light shone into my darkness. I guess I never realized how just a small glimmer of light could really make a difference in a dark, dark place. Elaine was the spark I knew I needed.

Living in the Light

Dividedness can only produce tension in your life, and it isn't pleasant. So, in order to live in the light and truly enjoy this journey called life, you must break this tension. I want you to think about the things in your life you are most prone to hide from your spouse, your friends, your family. Is it fears you have, anger, feelings of inadequacy, maybe various forms of shame? What are you holding inside that keeps you from fully connecting in your relationships? That is where the tension resides and that is where you must break through.

But too often we search for answers that make sense to us and don't come from God's perspective. We want immediate solutions, yet God is interested in eternal solutions. We want comfort, God wants character. We want to receive, God desires that we give. In your searching for answers to break the tension of dividedness in your life, do not ignore the truth God has for you. The truth will set you free.

Faking

Elaine and I started dating, which wasn't actually what I was angling for at first. After my relationship with Jess ended, I ranted against all women and spewed vile thoughts and words about how stupid relationships are and that it is useless to expect anything good from them. I even went so far as to make a vow that I would not kiss another girl until I put a ring on her finger. One month after making this rash vow, I met Elaine.

Our first date was at a restaurant called Mejor Que Nada (Spanish for "Better Than Nothing"). Despite its name, it was a great restaurant and we had a fantastic time. Elaine was nervous, as indicated by her untouched plate of food. But she was also engaging. She never seemed to be anything but genuine, in her speech or her mannerisms. It was quite refreshing, especially after having had some dating experiences where there was nothing but phoniness (on both sides of the table).

After dinner, I took Elaine down to the river and played my guitar and sang her a few songs I had recently written. We walked along the river and talked, eventually making our way back to my house to talk some more.

This first date fell on a significant day, September 23, the same day my dad had died two years earlier. I shared this fact with Elaine and even pulled out a letter Daddy had written me and read it to her. For some reason I felt totally at ease with Elaine in sharing these deeply personal parts of my life. I can't explain it other than I felt safe in the presence of a person who didn't project pretense or dividedness. She was gracious, considering this isn't exactly what one would expect for a first date. She was even a bit flattered that I would consider asking her out on such a significant anniversary. But I was interested in writing a new chapter in my life, and it seemed appropriate to let Elaine's light shine in on my darkness on that day.

******

Ah, a new chapter. Sounds refreshing, doesn't it? Like all the problems of my life fell away after my first encounter with this saintly girl Elaine, right? Not quite. While we did start seeing each other more regularly and eventually dated one another exclusively, I did not share my secret with her. Honestly, it never even occurred to me that I needed to share it. Elaine was a fresh start and I felt very positive about her influence in my life. I was more focused on how this new beginning could launch me in the right direction than I was about uncovering my secret, thinking that the new beginning alone would be enough to overcome any deficit brought about by the secret.

One of the great deceptions of Satan is distraction, getting us focused on that which has nothing to do with truth or healing. I was focused on a new beginning, which is a good thing, but it distracted me from revealing my dark secret and cleaning out the clutter of my sexual addiction and perfectionism. While it may seem noble and right to move forward in hope and determination, as long as the secret remained inside me there would be no progress toward real freedom and wholeness, either within me or in any of my relationships.

Elaine, however, really was a positive influence on my life, especially coming off the painful relationship with Jess the previous summer. Elaine made me want to be a better man. But wanting to be a better man and actually knowing how to go about doing it were two very different things. I, unfortunately, translated my desire to be a better man as needing to present myself as a better man, not actually learn what it meant to genuinely improve. Even so, it still felt like a move in the right direction, never mind the fact that this only perpetuated my dividedness and left Elaine to fall in love with only half a man, if that.

******

I was nervous. I had driven from San Angelo, in west Texas, to San Antonio to spend part of the Christmas break with Elaine and her family. Our dating relationship was really flourishing and I was growing more and more in love with her each day. I had never met anyone so pure and complete. I was finding out that what her eyes told me on that first day I met her was true: she was the real deal, genuinely caring, authentically beautiful. Now, I was going to meet her entire family and spend the most family-oriented holiday with them. Plus, I had something very important that I wanted to tell Elaine.

I had met Elaine's immediate family prior to Christmas, so I wasn't being thrown completely into the lion's den. But I hadn't met the rest of the family, and there were a lot of them. Grandparents, cousins, aunts, uncles, an unbelievable number of people. And that was just one side of Elaine's family! But in spite of all the people, the atmosphere was pleasant, light, and fun. Love flowed from room to room and the conversations were energetic and meaningful. I immediately felt at home among all these strangers, and they welcomed me pretty well too.

Food, football, music, and laughter were in abundance that Christmas. But after the festivities settled a bit I still had a mission to accomplish. I really needed to tell Elaine something, it was gnawing at my gut and I just kept looking for the right time to share it. The time came one evening when Elaine and I were alone outside her grandparents' house. We were walking to the car when I looked at her and told her I had something important to say. Then I said it.

"I love you, Elaine."

There are a few statements you make in life that come with a preconceived idea of what to expect in response. For instance, when a judge inquires of a jury "Have you reached a verdict?" you expect the foreman to respond "Yes." Or when you walk past a person and say "Hi, how are you?" you expect the bland (and often dishonest) reply "Fine." To say "I love you" to someone is a huge risk, like handing over the rope connected to the noose around your neck, gambling how the person will use this newly acquired leverage. I had an expectation of how I wanted Elaine to respond, and I think you could accurately guess what I expected.

Instead . . . silence. Elaine's response to my heartfelt, genuine expression of affection was to stand silent. I didn't know what to do. I felt my temperature rise, my palms moisten, and the back of my throat dry up like a west Texas creek bed. Finally, after a few more moments of awkward silence, Elaine explained why she did not give the standard, expected reply to my declaration of love for her. She shared that she was reserving those words only for the man she was certain to marry, and while I wasn't excluded from that potential list, she wasn't certain in her mind if I was that man (besides the fact that I hadn't yet asked her to marry me!). The explanation helped, but it didn't erase the discomfort of the moment. I didn't know what to do when my expectation wasn't met.

They say that maturity can be measured by how well a person responds to disappointment. When Elaine didn't reciprocate my "I love you" I was disappointed, perplexed really. And I had a long way to go to reach maturity (I still do). While I didn't show it on the outside, on the inside I was throwing a pity party, upset and embarrassed by my inability to have things work out the way I expected. A real childish way of thinking, I know. I mean, after all, it was only one tiny little conversation that didn't even end up in an argument, but I got all bent out of shape inside because Elaine wouldn't say "I love you." What a kid I was.

At this point it should be stated that I really didn't know how to grow healthy relationships (you might have figured this out on your own by now). My idea of a good relationship was one that went how I thought it should go, my expectations being met and my ideas being adopted. I didn't understand that part of a healthy relationship actually included talking about disappointments or negative emotions or points of disagreement or any sort of conflict of ideas. I didn't see working through such difficulties as being integral to a strong, growing relationship.

Therefore, whenever I would feel these negative emotions or disappointments (with myself, Elaine, or both), I would hide them and simply pretend I was OK. I would fake it, glossing over issues, playing the part I thought Elaine wanted to see, thus increasing my dividedness and hiding a little more of the real me behind the veil of my perfectionism. With all my mounting secrets, the prospect of a healthy relationship was quietly, and quickly, fading away.

******

"I am not a virgin."

These were the words I spoke to Elaine in the early spring months of 1995. It was the first time I had shared anything of my secret with anyone, and I was scared. I didn't know how Elaine would respond to this news, but I felt compelled to tell her because I was beginning to think that she might be "The One," and I didn't want to enter that level of relationship without sharing something of my hidden self. Although I wasn't ready to share the whole truth, I wanted her to know that I hadn't managed my sexuality perfectly. We were in a restaurant when I shared this part of my secret. Maybe on a subconscious level I believed that telling her in a public place might reduce any dramatic reactions she might have to such a hard blow. Not that Elaine had demonstrated any tendencies toward public outbursts, but you never know how a person might react when they are faced with potential "relationship-killer" news. So, I told her I wasn't a virgin. Then I waited.

I was beginning to notice a pattern in how Elaine responded to "heavy" news. She would pause, not quick to volley words. I also noticed that her eyes would squint just a touch, like she was processing the information and waiting for the read out to come across her mind before giving her answer. This was quite a chunk of information, so the wait seemed to me an eternity.

I can't recall the specific words Elaine used when she eventually did respond to my statement that day, but I do remember there being a several week "pause" in our dating after that meeting. It was like Elaine needed some additional time to process the magnitude of what I had revealed. It was certainly a heavy blow and I couldn't argue with her need for space. I knew such a reality would land hard and I just kept my fingers crossed that it wasn't a fatal blow to our growing relationship.

I also remember increased feelings of fear and shame during the days and weeks following my confession. Some moments I would feel panicky, like I just gave away the combination to the lock that protected my heart, questioning whether I made a good choice by telling Elaine my secret (at least part of it, anyway). At other times I would feel heavy with shame, regretting the very fact that I had such a secret to tell, imagining how "easy" love might be if I had made wiser choices in my past. Fear and shame, like squabbling cousins, badgered me over and over during those days.

A couple of weeks after my partial confession, Elaine asked to talk with me. I remember thinking this might be it, the moment Elaine lets me go, unwilling to move forward with a defiled man (and who could blame her?).

But Elaine surprised me. She shared with me that while my confession was a difficult blow, she loved me (yes, she said she loved me!), and that she wanted to press on in the relationship. She talked about how God had forgiven her of many sins in her past and given her multiple second chances, so she extended the same grace toward me. I was floored. I felt like I was floating around the room, like a prisoner walking past the iron bars, free from the shackles of guilt and shame. Well, a part of me felt this way, anyway.

When Elaine said she wanted to continue our relationship, two things happened. First, I knew I loved this woman and that she was truly the genuine article (way out of my league!). Her character of grace and mercy was unparalleled and she demonstrated such strength and resolve. I was amazed at her depth of feeling and willingness to press on. Second, however, was a conscious decision that nothing more of my secret would be revealed to Elaine—ever! The reasoning behind this was two-fold, yet with the same ultimate purpose: protection.

On the one hand I wanted to "protect" Elaine from going through the emotional anguish of again working through the ugliness of my dark deeds. Sounds noble, but totally irrational when you think about the point of a relationship being oneness.

On the other hand, my reasoning for locking away the secret for good was for my own protection. I didn't want any more of my hidden deeds messing up my plans to eventually marry Elaine. I figured if anything else about my secret came to the surface it would sink me for sure. So, the secret was buried deeper and my façade to the outside world was refined, especially toward Elaine.

I continued to smile on the outside, but on the inside I was depressed and sullen. But I was familiar and comfortable with the image I portrayed, and everyone else seemed to like it too. Therefore, I became content to become who I thought I should be, and leave the secret alone. Like they say, "Don't wake the sleeping giant." Being fake seemed easier, even though there was a small, gnawing whisper in my soul that kept hinting at the reality that someday the giant would awake, forcing me to engage it.

I chose not to listen to that voice.

Living in the Light

Maybe by now you are realizing you need to uncover some secrets in your life. That's good. But be careful of only telling pieces of the truth and not the whole truth. It is easy to deceive yourself into thinking that bringing one piece of your secret into the light is the same as bringing the whole thing out. It is not the same.

A fresh start is good, but it is only half of the equation when desiring to live in the light. The other half is emptying the closet of secrets in the dark. Anything you leave in the dark, especially in your marriage relationship, has the potential to draw you back into old, isolated patterns of thinking and behaving. You need to keep that closet clean, not stuffing any more secrets inside. Because the more secrets you carry the more you have to pretend in your relationships. And pretending will never satisfy because that which is fake can never adequately replace what is real.

Don't pretend any longer. Begin today to uncover the real you, all of him (or her).

Marriage Works!

I was on the phone one day with Elaine in March of 1995, she in her dorm room and I in mine. We were talking, laughing, just sharing about our day, our friends, our future. The "M" word came up: marriage. Elaine was so excited. We talked for a while about the possibility of marriage, enjoying what it felt like to share our thoughts and feelings about what that chapter might look like if we were to make such a commitment. The more we talked the more certain I became that Elaine was the only woman I wanted to spend the rest of my life with. In that phone conversation I became convinced she would be my wife. Now I just had to ask her!

In May, I set things up for me and Elaine to travel to Nashville so I could propose to her. (A friend of mine lived there, so I worked it out for us to stay at his place while there.) Elaine didn't know about the proposal (although it wasn't every day we were taking trips halfway across the country; I'm sure she had it somewhat figured out). We got to Nashville, spent the night at my friend's house, then set out the next day on my proposal adventure, which proved to be more of an adventure than I anticipated.

I took Elaine to Rio Bravo for lunch, where we actually saw Michael W. Smith in the buffet line with his son. I was praying Elaine wouldn't get too distracted by Michael to ruin what I was going to ask her later. He was, after all, quite an attractive guy. Nevertheless, we enjoyed a great meal in a very relaxed and pleasant atmosphere. When we exited the restaurant, we walked to my friend's car (he let us borrow it for the day). The doors were locked. I tried to unlock the doors with my friend's keys. Nothing. (My friend later told me that his keys quit working on the door locks about a year prior. This would have been helpful information.) I was a bit frustrated, but nothing was going to keep me from proposing to Elaine that day. I was on a mission.

My friend's car was a two-door sports car, and behind the front car door windows were other small, triangle-shaped windows. I pressed in on the triangular window on the driver's side, seeing that it gave a little. I then wondered if I could pry it open enough to reach a finger inside and unlock the door. As I increased pressure on the window, I was getting closer and closer to being able to get my hand inside to unlock the front door. With one more push, however, the window shattered and my hand flew through the glass, gashing my palm. It hurt, but I wasn't as concerned about my hand (or the window) as I was with continuing the mission of asking Elaine to marry me. We found some Band-Aids in the glove compartment and patched up my hand. The window wasn't so fortunate. It got tossed in the dumpster behind Rio Bravo.

Finally in the car and driving down the road, my hand bandaged enough to prevent it from bleeding on my friend's car, I continued with my plans to propose to Elaine. We arrived at a park I had scoped out earlier, Edwin Warner Park. (I have no idea who Edwin Warner was, but his park is nice.) We got out of the car and began hiking up the hills surrounding the park. It was a beautiful day, warm and sunny, with a gentle breeze dancing through the tall trees. As we hiked, Elaine got a few steps in front of me on a particular trail winding up the side of a hill. I knew this was my moment to make my move.

I quietly reached into my pocket where I had stashed her engagement ring. I slipped it over my pinky finger and then got Elaine's attention.

"Hey, Elaine."

Elaine turned around, "Yeah?"

"Do you know I love you?"

Elaine's face lit up with her priceless smile, her eyes beginning to dance. She took a few steps down the hill toward me, "Yes, I know you love me."

We embraced. It was a good hug, the kind that reminds you that true love is real and is meant to be felt from head to toe. As we pulled back slightly from the hug I looked her in the eye and casually said, "Oh, by the way. Will you marry me?" As I said those words, I lifted my hand carrying the ring on my finger so it was right in front of her face.

Elaine couldn't contain herself. She jumped into my arms on the side of that hill in Edwin Warner Park and squeezed me so tight I thought my head would pop off my shoulders. We smiled, laughed, looked deeply into each other's eyes. It was a memorable moment, one that will never leave me. Oh, and we kissed, our first kiss.

Elaine and I had dated for nine months without so much as touching lips. Remember, I made a vow not to kiss a girl until I put a ring on her finger. Well, the ring was on, so we kissed. And what a kiss it was! Have you ever had a moment in your life you would like to bottle up? This was such a moment. The air, the atmosphere, the thoughts, the touch, the love, everything about that moment was pure and perfect. It felt electric and even a bit eternal, like something spiritual was taking place. I cherish the memory of that moment.

We spent the rest of our time in Nashville enjoying being together, visiting different tourist attractions with my friend, and certainly sharing some more wonderful kisses.

******

After Elaine and I got engaged, we set a wedding date of December 30, 1995 (just in time to get the tax break!). Our engagement months seemed to fly by, at least they did in my mind. And I grew a bit more anxious during those months about my secret, the fact that there was still so much in the dark that Elaine knew nothing about. Pornography, masturbation, fantasies, and even a few "kissing friends" were still hidden from her. (I secretly kept in touch with a few old "girlfriends" for when the urge would strike me to want to make out.) I could feel my dividedness digging into my soul, but I didn't know what to do about it and I was certain I was not going to do anything to jeopardize my impending marriage to Elaine. I pushed this anxiety to the back burner and tried to focus on the positive direction my life could take once I got married.

The wedding day eventually came and it was a great day. It was held in a huge church in San Antonio, with more than enough space to accommodate the hundreds of people who attended. I was nervous, just like any groom to be, but I was also certain that I was doing the right thing. I knew Elaine was the girl for me and I truly loved her, and I wanted to make her happy. I had my doubts about whether I could accomplish that, but on that day I felt certain it was possible.

The ceremony was beautiful, and the reception was fun. After all the formalities, we drove away from that church and I was on cloud nine. I distinctly remember feeling like an "adult" at that moment, like I somehow transferred from child to grown-up in that moment we were declared "man and wife." I also remember the subtle feeling of not having a clue what it meant to actually be an adult, but I figured if anybody could fake being an adult, I could. But all those thoughts got immediately pushed to the side later that evening when we checked into our hotel room. There were more pressing matters at hand, matters that will not be divulged in this book.

******

Did you know marriage cures a man's problem with lust? It does. And there was none happier than I for discovering this wonderful news. I had searched so long for an answer to my decade-long struggle with lust and pornography, and finally the answer was found. I just needed to get married! What a relief. At least for the first month, anyway.

Yes, the cure was short-lived. And it wasn't Elaine's fault that marriage didn't cure my lust problem. She was wonderful, satisfying, and everything I could have hoped for in a wife. But my secret didn't care about her. My secret existed long before I met Elaine and demanded things that no woman could satisfy. In fact, that's really what the secret taught me, that lust is never satisfied. So, after only a few weeks of marriage, the old feelings of lust and fantasy began to resurface.

At first, I didn't think too much of my acting out. It seemed normal and unimportant, not so terrible that it would threaten my new marriage. A look at a magazine, a moment of masturbation in the shower, a brief fantasy. These just didn't seem like behaviors that would topple my marriage. After all, I wasn't engaging in these behaviors because I was dissatisfied with Elaine, I just wanted to have some fun for myself, with myself. I didn't see any danger in these seemingly insignificant behaviors.

But what I couldn't see was that these behaviors were only the bread crumbs I had left on the trail, the trail that led back to the secret, where the sleeping giant was stirring.

Living in the Light

What are you looking to as the "solution" to your inner struggle with lust, pride, fear, or anger? Have you believed that marriage would cure your struggle with lust? Or maybe you thought landing the "perfect" job would relieve your anxieties about money? It is easy to look to certain circumstances in hopes they will "cure" our inner dysfunctions and struggles. But they won't.

Living in the light will require looking beyond your circumstances and dealing with the roots of your pain and your wrong thinking. A spouse or a job or a new house or any other "thing" won't fix your problems with lust, greed, anger, or selfishness. And the longer you keep searching for relief and freedom in those things, the longer you will remain divided and dissatisfied.

Begin to reshape your thinking about where you are looking for solutions to your inner struggles. Stop looking around and start looking up. You just might find the solution is closer than you think, from one who "sticks closer than a brother."

Stepping Off the Cliff

Secrets don't usually destroy a person overnight. The process is much more subtle. Most people who end up in drug rehab clinics or walking street corners begging for food don't get there due to one bad decision or one unlucky break. No, a trip to the bottom is often a slow one, marked by winding trails of clever temptations that bear no obvious, or immediate, threat to a person's life. This was how my secret grew, little by little over many years. With each seemingly inconsequential invitation to exercise my lust, I was slowly, but certainly, being destroyed from the inside out. And I didn't even know how great a destruction it would be.

******

One day Elaine came home from work to discover me playing with my newest toy: a computer. Her expression was a mixture of shock and confusion, like she had missed out on something that should have been a joint venture. And she did miss out. You see, I hadn't talked with her about it, just decided I wanted it, and so I bought it with a credit card. This was another illustration of my total ineptitude at adulthood and building healthy relationships. My paradigm for life was self-centered, and this began to reveal itself clearly in my young marriage.

Shortly after purchasing the computer, I got connected to the Internet. This was when the Internet was fairly new, so the quality of technology was very primitive compared to today. A simple dial-up connection was all I had to connect to the information superhighway. Regardless, it wasn't long before I was conducting searches for pornography, and finding it. I didn't even care that it took thirty minutes to download one porn picture, I was hooked and the secret was coming alive again.

The challenge, however, to my new, and growing, hunger for pornography was that I was now married. This wasn't merely a moral dilemma, but one of practicality. I had to become more secretive and cunning in my searches, viewing, and acting out behaviors. In other words, I had to get better at lying to my wife, whether it be about searching for porn online or thumbing through a magazine or ordering a video (these were all part of my rituals at the time). And I did become more skilled at lying and hiding, but not without the consequence of increased inner tension and guilt.

I remember one occasion early in our marriage when my guilt overwhelmed me and I confessed to Elaine that I had looked at a Victoria's Secret catalog and fantasized over the models. She took the news pretty well, even thinking it was noble of me to confess such a "common" struggle. What I failed to tell her, however, was that I was also looking at full nudity online and masturbating to these images as well. It was like a part of me wanted to come clean, but not so much as to reveal the whole truth. The secret had such power over me, I was even losing my ability to recognize the truth.

But life went on. I had a job, Elaine was still in college. Our days were just like everyone else's, filled with tasks and responsibilities and deadlines. And, at that time, my secret didn't seem to overwhelm me. I wasn't feeling any immediate effects of my increasing porn use. In fact, I really didn't know what to look for as "signs" of developing a sexual addiction. It's not like you reach a magic number of "hits" and cross over this imaginary line into addiction. Addiction acts more like a crop of weeds that slowly and persistently grows up around your soul, choking your life from the inside out. And these weeds only grow in the dark, in the secret places, where no one else can see them—not even you.

My Internet use gradually increased over that first year of marriage. As my use grew so did my delusional thoughts about life, marriage, relationships, women, and any other aspect of real life. Porn and fantasy only filled my mind with lies, detestable thoughts and ideas that had no basis in reality or truth. Truly, the saddest part about my slide down the spiral of sexual addiction was that I wasn't aware of the descent. I just kept sliding, oblivious (in my conscious mind) to the hell that awaited me. And even though I knew the behaviors I engaged in were wrong, I didn't fully understand the scope of the collective destruction they would eventually bring to my life. I kept seeing each individual sin (viewing a porn image online, spinning a single sexual fantasy, masturbation, etc.) as disconnected from all the others, like they were independent of one another and therefore wouldn't "build up" against me.

Stress and tension mounted in our home and in our relationship. Poor Elaine didn't have a clue of the origin of the growing tension; she only knew that there was this chasm slowly widening between us. At that point in our relationship, however, she didn't deduce that such tension was anything unusual for a newly married couple. She figured this was just part of the marriage "hiccups" that every couple faces in their first year.

I was still unwilling to acknowledge that I was addicted to porn and felt no desperation concerning my secret behaviors. The truth is that nobody wants to admit they are an addict. The label carries with it shame and ridicule, as if you are odd, different from the rest of humanity. I knew I liked the momentary pleasure of viewing porn, but I also hated the resulting feelings of disgust, shame, and fear. I would regularly confess to God my secret sinful behaviors, feeling cleansed and renewed, yet never free. I continued hiding new secrets, which only aided in perpetuating this cycle over and over.

I changed jobs about nine months into our marriage, working as the manager of a convenience store. This change only reinforced and accelerated my addiction. This was a place where hundreds of people revolved in and out every day, people of all types and all backgrounds. The general mood of most people who frequented the store was one of depression, frustration, and hopelessness ("Another day, another dollar, with no end in sight"). The whole atmosphere in the store just felt dark to me, and is there any better place to keep secrets than in the dark?

The dark mood of my workplace started to expand to my home and marriage. The convenience store business is highly competitive and requires very long hours from those in management. My days would start well before 6 a.m. and sometimes extended late into the evening. That alone would have proven enough of a strain on my marriage and personal health. But it was the dark mood more than anything that caused the real damage. I began to feed off the depression and angst of my customers, believing that life should be fair to me and that any discomfort should be medicated in some way for immediate relief. Before long, I too believed (on a subconscious level) the world must revolve around me and that my desires must be met at all cost, no matter how trivial or childish or sexual.

Emotionally, I stepped off a cliff into the dark. I can't recall a specific date or time when this occurred, but it happened in that first year of marriage. Maybe it happened a little every day, I don't know. All I do know is that the secret pulled me back into the pit and began leading me by the hand into territory I had never dreamed of entering. But that is the nature of addiction, drawing us into thoughts and behaviors we firmly believed we would never think or do. As I stepped off the ledge, a piece of my soul was lost, as if the darkness consumed me and I was unable to find my way back to a place of peace and sanity. I had no idea how far the fall would be, or if I would ever be able to stand again.

> If either of them falls down, one can help the other up. But pity anyone who falls and has no one to help them up. (Ecclesiastes 4:10)

Living in the Light

The longer you keep secrets the more you become isolated and disconnected from reality. This disconnection can foster a lot of crazy thoughts and ideas. You can even become delusional in your thinking, believing that you don't have any problems regardless of the mounting evidence to the contrary. It is these delusional thoughts and patterns that must be brought into the light if you want to experience a truly abundant life, a life of peace and sanity.

Is there anything you do in your life that you minimize? Are you regularly looking at porn, lying to your spouse or friends, cutting corners at work, or doing anything that you don't want anyone else to know about? Do you justify or rationalize these behaviors, convincing yourself they "aren't that big a deal?" If so, you have a problem and it needs to come into the light. Don't fall any further into the trap of isolation and delusion. Connect today with your spouse or a few friends and invite them to help you out of your pit of self-deception.

Racing to the Bottom

My delusions increased in the second year of marriage. My unhappiness grew exponentially as I immersed myself more deeply into Internet pornography and lustful fantasies. My patterns of acting out became more regular and demanding. I felt less and less control over my sexuality, my rational mind being driven more and more by the darkness of my secret. I believed the lies my sexual lust was telling me, that my marriage was a mistake and that I had to find a way out. But how?

I began spending more time on the computer, more time on the Internet. Most of my time on the Internet would eventually lead to seeking out pornography. Porn, however, was beginning to bore me, not producing the same kind of thrill it once did, even though I had "progressed" to more hard-core pictures. I was experiencing what is known as the law of diminishing returns, which means that in order for a person to experience the same level of stimulation, more "drug" is needed. The same ole porn just wasn't doing it for me. Then I discovered chat.

Chat technology had just been introduced within months of me getting connected to the Internet, and I was hooked. Until I began chatting, I always had to create sexual fantasies based off a static image on a magazine page or computer screen or just dream them up in my own mind. Now, with chat, I was introduced to other people's fantasies and could mingle them with my own. This sort of "cyber sex" increased the thrill of my online activities. It gave me a rush to get online, join a chat group, and begin the "hunt" for a compatible cyber partner.

My times in the chat rooms accelerated my frustrations and discontent with my marriage. I was being fed all sorts of lies about marriage, love, sex, fidelity and so on. After all, when you're online in a chat room having sexual conversations with a stranger, you aren't exactly there to tell the truth to each other. My secret was growing, the giant was stirring, and I was picking up speed on my way to rock bottom.

******

Without speaking a word, I meticulously packed my Ford Escort to the gills with all my belongings (at least all the ones I wanted to take with me). With anger, frustration, confusion, and fear as my motivators I kept stuffing the car with worthless possessions; fax machine, files, toolbox, even Band-Aids. One possession I ensured was onboard was the computer. With the car loaded, and the gas tank full, I pulled out of the parking lot of our apartment complex and drove away, leaving behind my cares, my worries, and my wife.

I didn't really know what I would find (or even what I was looking for) out on the open road. I just knew I had to get away, to escape all that seemed to be pressing in on my secret, demanding that I make a choice; either it or a different life. I didn't want to face that choice, so I escaped. I always ran. (I still want to run sometimes.) The problem, however, with running was that no matter how far I ran away, I was still there. And the problem I so desperately wanted to run from resided in me.

Sexual addiction really is about escape, running away from all that is not comfortable or convenient. There is certainly more to it in terms of its complexity and how it manifests itself in different people, but ultimately it drives a person to escape pain. What the sex addict doesn't understand, however, is that continuing to medicate the pain with secret sexual behaviors only increases the agony. In my attempt to escape pain, I only invited more in.

I eventually landed in Nashville and crashed at an old college buddy's house. He agreed to take me in on a temporary basis, not really knowing what to do with me or how to counsel me in my situation. Looking back, I can see what an awkward position this put him in and how frustrating it must have been for him to have me taking up space in his place while he was trying to get work done, sleep, eat, etc.

I was a mess. I attempted to look for a job, but really just wanted to hang out by the pool and wallow in my self-pity and anger. I was a very angry person, frustrated at how "difficult" life had to be and that it ultimately demanded I think of others and not only myself. That especially angered me!

So, I put some feelers out for work, swam a little in the afternoons, periodically thought about what my next move would be, and always landed on the computer before the day was done. I had begun to develop several ongoing chat relationships and felt compelled to stay in touch, even as my life was falling apart.

I had no contact with Elaine during this time. My mother called me several times to try and "talk me down," to fix the situation. I also had some other friends call in attempts to talk sense into me, appealing to my people-pleaser tendencies. I answered some of the calls, but even so I never really listened to what they were trying to tell me.

After a couple weeks of nothing, tension began to surface between me and my friend. He didn't come right out and tell me to take a hike, but I could tell he was growing tired of my intrusion. I too was growing tired of the illusion I was searching for, knowing deep down that I would never find peace when I was a thousand miles away from home. By the beginning of my third week away, I realized the foolishness of my escape and headed home. I wondered if there would still be a wife waiting for me when I returned.

******

A Band-Aid was never designed to hold back the flow of Niagara Falls. This picture describes what marriage counseling was like for me and my wife upon my return from Nashville. Elaine graciously, yet understandably cautiously, received me back home. We agreed to get some marriage counseling. It just seemed like the appropriate thing to do. We had no idea how much trouble our marriage was actually in, primarily because I still refused to be completely transparent in the sessions, along with the fact that our counselor was ill-equipped to handle our particular situation.

Regardless of the fact that counseling didn't do much, our relationship did improve. I focused on being a "good husband." I genuinely wanted to experience what I had always only imagined in my mind, that feeling of adulthood, confidence, and security. For six months after my return, I held it all together pretty well. But I never let the secret, the whole secret, go. And this proved to be my ultimate undoing.

It also didn't help matters that I filed for bankruptcy just prior to our second anniversary. Secret addiction affects every area of your life, not just what seems most obvious.

******

Shortly after the bankruptcy was completed, we moved to San Antonio. We were both ready for a fresh start (sound familiar?) and San Antonio would put us closer to family. We moved without either one of us having a job. We lived in Elaine's parent's house until we were able to get jobs and secure an apartment. This created some stress in our relationship and I was again relieving my stress through misusing my sexuality (mostly masturbation at this point).

The following year was truly hell on earth (as Elaine put it). I went headlong into my Internet addiction and developed multiple online relationships with women in chat rooms. I was obsessed with spending time online writing out fantasies and reading the twisted thoughts of others. Then, one day while chatting, it happened.

"Wanna meet?"

The cursor on the screen just hung there blinking below the question. Prior to that moment, all my online interactions were just that, online. Now this question comes across that is challenging me to cross yet another bold barrier into a deeper realm of darkness and secrecy. I barely hesitated.

"Yes."

There is a passage in the Bible that talks about a man who committed an atrocious sexual sin, and the apostle Paul addressed the issue by instructing the church to "hand this man over to Satan, so that the sinful nature may be destroyed" (1 Corinthians 5:4–5). I believe, in a sense, my affirmative response to meet with this anonymous woman was the point at which I was given over to my lust, handed over to Satan, if you will. I didn't consciously realize it at the moment, but my spirit went dark on that day.

I met with the woman and committed adultery (I had committed adultery a thousand times before by my lust, but never physically). I stepped over a threshold, a cavernous precipice that raised the stakes exponentially on the fragility of the secret I carried. If I were to expose my secret now, it would surely be the end of me and my marriage.

This encounter opened the door to multiple similar affairs. Thankfully, much of my memory of these encounters is blurred, as if a clouded window has been lowered over them in my mind.

(I wouldn't share details even if my memory were clear.) But with each encounter, my will to fight, my desire for what was true and right, dissipated like dew that vanishes in the sun's heat. I also felt my soul withering, my life slowly fading away. It is quite hard to explain if you have never experienced the strangling power of a secret addiction. It grips your heart and squeezes out any life within, regardless of whether it takes a year, a decade or a lifetime.

Obviously, I now had to hide much more from Elaine. I was juggling more than I could handle. But I was still juggling. I lied. I blew up whenever accused. I was filled with rage, unable to control my outbursts of anger and frustration. My emotional self was ticking like a time bomb, ready to explode at any moment. I carried the deadly combinations of fear, anger, confusion, anxiety, shame, and desperation. I knew I couldn't hold the secret forever, but I also knew I couldn't tell anyone. I knew if I told anyone my secret, I would die. If I had been a wiser man, I would have realized that I was already dying.

For the wages of sin is death (Romans 6:23).

Living in the Light

One of the greatest lies you can believe is this: "If anyone knew the real me, they would completely reject me." Yet, this lie is what often causes us to keep hiding terrible secrets that are destroying us from the inside out.

What are you carrying, if anything, that you believe would cause someone you love to reject you if they knew about it? Is it an affair? Is it porn? Is it drugs, alcohol, or some other substance you run to in hopes it will medicate your inner pain? Whatever it is, it must eventually come out if you want to live in the light and have no more regrets. The hardest part about the process of bringing into the light the things you hold in the dark is that you might actually experience rejection from those you love.

Your worst nightmare might come true—for a season. But to even have the opportunity of experiencing deep love and true intimacy, the secret must come out. Otherwise, the best you can hope for is what you are experiencing now, and you have seen how well that is working. The choice is yours.

The End . . . Almost

Have you ever carried a secret that you knew you couldn't keep? Are you carrying that secret right now? Then you know, just like I did, that a day is coming when the secret meets the light of day. It no longer resides in the dark. It can't. You think you know what that day will be like, but you actually don't have a clue. I didn't, anyway.

By the summer of '99, the weight of my secret was crushing me. I couldn't hold it all together. My juggling act was failing. Information was slipping through the cracks. Pieces of paper with girl's names and phone numbers were found by Elaine and she would ask about them. I would forget to erase websites on the computer and they would pop up when Elaine was online. I couldn't balance the multiple lies that I was telling Elaine (and others) on a regular basis. I was wearing down. My time was up. Well, almost up.

Eventually, I didn't want to hold it all together anymore. I was tired of carrying the burden of dividedness and shame. I decided I would tell Elaine everything. Everything. I remember the night of my confession. Elaine was sitting on the couch. I was in my recliner, catty-corner to the couch. I can't remember exactly how the conversation started, but eventually I was tossing lethal bombs of secret information at Elaine. I told her about the Internet. I told her about chatting. I told her about the affairs. I unloaded the full arsenal of sexual secrets, leaving nothing in the dark. As I was lobbing these emotional bombs on my wife, I remember her slowly doubling over on the couch, tears streaming down her face. With each new piece of the secret tearing through her emotional being, she would curl up a little more, until eventually she was in a tight fetal position, unable to move, incapable of producing any more tears.

I had a very strange reaction to the confession, one I wasn't expecting. I felt better, relieved actually. I felt like a great weight had been lifted off my shoulders. I wasn't carrying the secret anymore. Unfortunately, I was too emotionally numb and self-centered at the time to see that every pound of the weight of my secret had landed squarely on the shoulders of my poor wife. It was an odd combination of feelings, though—relieved from not carrying the secret, yet numb to the effects my confession had on Elaine. I chose mainly, of course, to focus on the relief, thus believing my confession had set me free. This, however, was foolish, hasty and naïve thinking.

I experienced a principle of truth that night that I wouldn't actually learn until sometime later. The truth I learned was that confession alone changes nothing, unless it is combined with brokenness and repentance. I had confessed my secret sin and that was a good thing, like opening a door to a new possibility, but I was not broken over it. I was not yet to a point of helpless-ness, acknowledging that I could never live a life of fulfillment and joy and purity on my own. That lesson would have to come later.

The confession was a rough night, to say the least. We eventually went to bed and got up the next day and went through our normal routine of daily life; work, home, eat, sleep. What boggled my mind was that nothing seemed to change. I still had the same job. I still lived in the same house. I still had the same wife (for the moment, anyway). I still had the same body and so on. In a sense, it reminded me of my salvation experience in my grandmother's bathroom. Nothing big happened. No bolt of lightning jolted me free from lust, no angel delivered a message of hope to me and my wife that everything would be OK, and I especially didn't feel any different. Life just went on like it always had, too much like it always had.

By about Thursday of the following week I was online again and I wasn't checking stock quotes. I was on the hunt. Soon I found a willing partner, a woman I had seen before. We made arrangements to meet that Saturday morning. I was a ball of nerves for the next twenty-four hours. I knew I had just stuffed away a new secret in the dark, even after unloading them all less than a week before. I realized I had time to stop this encounter, but my fear and cowardice were overpowering and I refused to tell anyone. Saturday morning came and I snuck out of the house while Elaine was in the shower. I met the woman, had sex, and then drove home in silence and overwhelming shame.

I learned then, during my agonizing drive home, that confession alone changes nothing. Simply being honest wasn't enough. Why did my confession not change anything? What would it take to bring me to a place of change, a point of real transformation where my heart didn't feel black and calloused all the time? I was a mess, panicky and shaking as I drove home. The rush of sex was so short-lived and each encounter brought less and less relief from the shame and despair I felt.

I was also very scared on that drive home for another reason. Not only had I become irrational in my ever-increasing pursuit of sex, I had also become unsafe. This last encounter was the second time in a row that I engaged in unprotected sex, exposing myself to who knows how many possibilities of disease. As I drove, I wondered if I would be the next victim of HIV or some other sexually transmitted disease. My heart sank and I just wanted to die, to literally die.

✶✶✶✶✶✶

I grew up in church. I had heard hundreds of testimonies from people whose lives were a mess, whether it was drugs, alcohol, or whatever else, and that God set them free when they came to the end of themselves. I would listen to these stories, amazed yet skeptical. You see, I never knew anyone personally with such a story. All my Christian friends were pretty well polished, and the few unbelieving friends I had weren't too scuffed up themselves. So, whenever I heard a "rags to riches" testimony, I couldn't understand how a person's life could get so messed up, especially from those who lived in America. And I knew I would never relate to such stories.

But for thirteen years I had been dying. I hadn't been dying physically (although, I suppose each day we are closer to death than the day before). No, I had been dying on the inside, emotionally and spiritually. I became acquainted with the monster of lust, although he didn't seem so threatening and scary when I was a kid. But thirteen years later, he had grown into a horrible beast, tightening his stranglehold to squeeze the last breath of life from me. My inner man was barely alive, unaware that I actually needed to die if I was ever going to live. I needed to give up in order to win.

During all my years of addiction, whenever the shame of my sin or the pain of its consequences would arise, I would ultimately try to find a solution on my own. Sure, I prayed and went to church and even occasionally asked for some help, but it was all with the mind-set of "fixing" my problem. I never once considered living a new life, a different life, a Christ-led life. Rather, I just wanted my struggle with lust to disappear so I could go on living my life as I saw fit. God, however, had a different plan, a better plan, the best plan, even if it would cost me my life.

******

I pulled my car up to the house. I walked slowly to the front door, my head hanging. I stopped at the front door, took a deep breath, and turned the knob. As I walked through the door, my inner man breathed his last.

> Then Jesus said to his disciples, "Whoever wants to be my disciple must deny themselves and take up their cross and follow me. For whoever wants to save their life will lose it, but whoever loses their life for me will find it." Matthew 16:24–25

Living in the Light

Are you broken and repentant over your secret sins? Or are you simply wanting your problems "fixed" so you can keep moving forward in your life along the path you choose? This is an important distinction to make. Many of us want to have our cake and eat it too. We don't want the pain of our secret, selfish choices, but we don't want to relinquish control of our lives fully to God.

I often ask men struggling with sexual addiction if they want to be free. Their immediate response is "Yes!" But then I ask them if they are saying they want to simply be free from the consequences of their addictive behaviors or if they really want to be free to a life of purity and wholeness. They are often silent, pondering the question.

It is OK to want to be free from all the pain and dividedness we experience from living a double life of secrets. But until we reach the point where we want to be free to start a whole new life, one marked by surrender and obedience to God, we will never experience abundant life. A life lived in the light is one that desires good more than it desires simply being rid of bad.

Doors

Elaine's bags were packed when I walked through the door on that fateful Saturday. She told me she knew where I had been, that she found a slip of paper with a phone number on it after I left. She called the number and a woman answered. Elaine asked the woman if she knew me. The woman denied it, even though she was, in fact, the woman I went to see. Elaine didn't buy the woman's denial, then proceeded to tell me she was finished. She was through with my lies, through with the pain, and although she didn't know what she would do next, she couldn't stay in the house any longer. She packed up her car and drove away.

I am going to tell you something that will prove my insanity at the time (I truly believe my addiction was making me crazy, delusional). This isn't easy to say, because it will confirm with overwhelming certainty the degree to which I was a jerk and self-centered prick. OK, are you ready? Here goes.

I never believed Elaine would leave me.

It's true. Even as I was engaging in multiple affairs, lying daily to her, and becoming increasingly more difficult to live with, I never thought she would pack up and leave. But now I stood in the doorway of our house, watching her car fade away down the street, and I believed. Yet I continued to stand there, frozen, even after I couldn't see her car anymore. Eventually, I turned inside and closed the door.

As I stepped inside, I felt very alone—and scared. There was a deafening silence that ripped through the house, the only noise coming from the sound of my shallow, panicked breathing. It seemed as if the life had left, and in some ways it did. Elaine brought life to our tiny home. She held it together with her strength and character. Now that she was gone, so was the life.

But life leaving was just what I needed to bring me to the end of myself, truly to that place of rock bottom. Elaine left, and leaving with her were my delusions of continuing a double life. My inner man had wasted away and I wondered if I would ever breathe again, ever inhale the true breath of life. All seemed stale, bitter, and tasteless in that moment. Standing in the entryway, I looked around at that empty house. Its stillness, silence, and cold, hard edges spoke clearly of what my life had become: empty. The beast, it seemed, had won.

I walked slowly over to the couch and sat down. I placed my elbows on my knees and dropped my head into my hands in despair. I let out a long, exasperated sigh. What now? What would I do now?

I sat silently on the couch for a long time, wringing my hands and combing my fingers through my hair, searching for an answer. I kept hearing Elaine's car speeding off, her words of pain and anger echoing in my ears. My chest hurt, my body was tired, but I was too numb for tears. My mind was drifting all over the place, unable to concentrate on the intensity of the moment. The sound of the front door closing kept repeating over and over again in my mind, growing louder and louder with each swing, reminding me of all the lost opportunities during my marriage and over my lifetime because of my secret. "Enough!"

I got up from the couch and began walking around the living room. I was growing agitated with the constant reminders around me of all my failures as a man, as a husband. As I circled the living room, my eyes kept glancing over at the front door. I kept staring at the door, as if I could somehow make all my history of lies and secrets vanish by simply staring a hole through it. But the longer I stared, the more my mind shifted from my past to my future. That closed, locked door seemed to only represent my failures, my secret, my past. But the more I stared at it, I began to see that door as a passageway to my future, one that might possibly be different, even better. In that moment, I had my first clear thought in thirteen years, and it opened a new door to a future I never could have imagined.

******

In my mind, I saw a road with a fork in it. Each fork in the road represented a decision I could make regarding the rest of my life. It seemed a simple enough exercise, but my mind and body were tired, and I just didn't know if I had the energy to concentrate. I wondered momentarily if I would fail this test too, as I had all the previous.

One fork in the road, the one that went left, only required that I continue living life as I had. Self in the center, pleasure my idol, lies my method. I was familiar with this road, traveling it came naturally to me. But as I looked down that road it only lead to places called Death or Prison. And at that point in my life, death was coming sooner than prison. Something I haven't mentioned up to this point in my story is that several times in the year previous to Elaine leaving I came very close to killing myself. A few times, when Elaine wasn't home, I sat on the end of our bed with a loaded gun in my hand, pointing it at my head, trying to think of one good reason not to pull the trigger. Sometimes I sat there a long time. Thankfully, a reason to live always came to mind, even if it was a silly or simple one.

Looking down the other fork in the road took me back to when I was six years old in my grandmother's house. You remember that story, right? I remembered when I bowed my head next to Granny's toilet and asked Jesus to save me. As I recalled this significant moment, a tidal wave of tears erupted from my eyes. I saw clearly the choice I had to make, the choice to hand over the reins of my broken, pitiful life to the One who saved me so many years ago. I fell to the living room floor face-down, unable to stop the seemingly unending flow of tears. I sobbed and sobbed and sobbed. I had finally come to the point of brokenness. I finally came to the road called Life, the fork that could lead me home.

I felt God speaking to my heart in that moment of broken-ness. It was as if he was sighing, "Oh, Jonathan, I have waited a long time for this moment. I have been here all along. I never left you, even as you were pushing away from me. I love you. I'm proud of you for breaking open and letting me in." And with that, I began pouring out my heart in confession and bro-kenness to God. Years of unconfessed sin came to the surface, and with each confession I felt as though I was reaching over and dropping the filth of my sin into the toilet, the one next to which God saved me. Hours went by, the carpet was soaked with my tears. That day, as horrible as it started, ended with the most cleansing spiritual experience of my life.

I eventually lifted my head from the floor, my eyes swollen and red from weeping. I stood up, took in a deep breath, and felt my spirit leap within me. I looked around. The house was still empty, silent, and still. Elaine was still gone. My past was unchanged, but *life* now filled me and this gave me hope to travel on.

Living in the Light

Pain is the pathway to true peace. Don't believe anything less. Too often we deceive ourselves into thinking that a life of peace and contentment will come easily, without any struggle or anguish. Not so. Freedom, peace, and real satisfaction in life are only born out of pain. And to expose the real you when you have been carrying secrets is painful.

But the pain you experience in confessing your faults and failures is not a pain without purpose. It isn't painful simply for the sake of being painful. It is a pain that is leading somewhere, somewhere you actually have wanted to go for a long time. This pain breaks the dividedness of living a double life and brings opportunities to truly connect in your relationships without holding anything back. The real you emerges out of this pain.

In all this, God is present, he is near. When you cry out to God and admit you don't have it all together, that your life is a mess and you need help, he hears your cries. He is close to the brokenhearted, the ones who stop hiding who they really are and what they really struggle with day in and day out. So, stop hiding, confess your sins, embrace your brokenness, and look forward to the new day that is dawning in your life.

Baby Steps

Brokenness changed me. It was like I saw my life from a distance, a new objective point of view. I saw the secrets and lies for what they were, masks covering the real me, the wounded, scared, broken me. That day on the floor of my living room changed me. And I received something from God that I didn't expect: grace.

A lot of Christians talk about grace in flowery terms and lofty language as if God carries this magic wand that has been dipped in "grace" and if he simply chooses to wave it over you all your troubles will be over. And grace is often spoken of like it is available to anyone, but when the truly wretched dare to show up at church on Sunday, it's like grace flew out the stained glass window and that person is pounded with all the rules they must follow to be accepted. But I have come to realize that grace is available to anyone, even the stray child of God who spent years seeking to serve himself at the expense of everyone he loves. God's grace overshadowed my sin and rebellion. And it was just that grace that changed me, and it is that same grace that keeps changing me.

I think too often we are afraid of telling other people the truth about God's grace. We are afraid that if we tell someone God loves them and that nothing they have ever done or ever will do can change that fact, that person will immediately run off and do every despicable deed known to man. But I believe such fear shows a real lack in understanding the immeasurable, and powerful, grace of God, the kind of grace that will always stretch farther than our sin. When a person is touched by this sort of grace, he doesn't want to turn against the One who offers it. Instead, he wants to obey and serve the great Giver of such unbelievable kindness.

******

"If nothing changes, nothing changes." (Alcoholics Anonymous phrase)

The following week after Elaine left I set up an appointment with a counselor to get started on a recovery plan that would help me become a different man, a man of purity. The counselor set me up with a solid support group and thus began my road to recovery. I was enthusiastic, yet nervous about what might lie ahead on this journey. But I knew, I really knew, that God was for me. He was daily whispering words of affirmation and encouragement into my spirit as I embraced my new disciplines of walking in purity.

At first, all the changes were very uncomfortable and awkward. I felt like a three-year-old trying to operate a Harley Davidson motorcycle. This territory of being honest with other men, bearing my soul to a counselor, praying daily, resisting temptation (seemingly every second of the day!), it all seemed so foreign and unnatural. I suppose it should have felt unnatural. After all, for the previous thirteen years I had not been practicing these disciplines (at least not to the degree I was now). But I still had much to learn about what it meant to live a life of purity and not merely appear to live a life of purity.

******

I went 107 days in recovery without acting out. I hadn't gone two days in a row in the prior year without engaging in some sort of sexual acting out behavior, whether it was masturbation, pornography, fantasy, or some other mismanagement of my sexuality. This was quite an extraordinary accomplishment for me. I was feeling stronger each day of my recovery. I was regularly attending support groups, meeting with my counselor, and gaining incredible insight into God and his character. Then there was day 108.

I cannot remember any of the specific details of day 108, other than the fact that on that day I acted out. I masturbated. I panicked, thinking that all was lost in my recovery. I thought there was no way that I could go on because I had failed at being able to resist the temptations that led to my slip. I remember nervously sharing my failure with my counselor, very concerned about what his response might be to this colossal downfall. (I was certain that I was the only client he ever had that acted out during his recovery.) But my counselor stunned me with his response. He offered me the same response of grace that God had offered me when I came clean about my secret. I was speechless. I didn't know how to receive a response to my sin that wasn't condemning or shaming. It was as if my counselor understood my struggle and wanted to truly help me rather than shake his head and throw another cliché or rule at me.

Up through day 107 in my recovery journey I believed that purity equaled perfection. I learned something new, however, after day 108. I began to learn that my pursuit of purity was a journey of progression, undergirded by the gentle, yet strong, grace of God. I didn't have to be perfect! What a relief. I felt the weight of perfectionism and legalism fall from my spirit in that counseling session. I felt I had been given permission to try, to journey one step at a time, not bound by fear of failure, but rather spurred on by love and grace to get better day by day.

Ironically, I felt empowered, along with feeling loved and free, truly free.

My counselor used a wonderful, simple illustration to teach this lesson of progression to me. He asked me if I had ever been a baby. Duh! Of course I had. He then asked if I came out of the womb walking. Double duh! Of course not, no one does. Finally, he asked me how it was that I could walk into his office that day. What changed from the time I was born to now? (The light bulb started to flicker above my head.)

He continued, "Did you learn to walk the first time you tried? No. How about the second time? Probably not. How many hundreds of times do you think you fell down, scraped a knee, bloodied your nose, or hit your head before you learned to balance yourself well enough to walk?" (The light bulb was now fully lit.)

"That," he said, "is the mind-set you must have if you are ever going to effectively move toward walking in purity. It is a journey of steps, one at a time, over time, that ultimately leads to greater purity. But this purity isn't based on your ability, but rather it is based on your willingness to surrender to Christ, the one who lived the perfect, pure life, and allow his Spirit to live through yours."

My recovery blossomed from that point. I was finally inhaling the breath of life; I was embracing life in a way I never had before. For the first time in my life I truly felt alive. I didn't have to lie to cover anything up. There was nothing to cover up! The real me, with all his imperfections and deficiencies, was out in the open for all to see. And this freedom, this transparency, brought me peace and comfort I had never known, even in the midst of my dire circumstances. Even in my loneliness each night as I fell asleep, eyes fixed on the empty pillow next to me. The peace of God truly does surpass all understanding.

******

When Elaine left she moved in with her parents. I only saw her once after that. About a week after she left, she came by the house to pick up the remainder of her belongings. We only spoke briefly and it wasn't pleasant. There were no fireworks, no angry words, but the encounter was flat and lifeless. It was awkward and uncomfortable for both of us.

The only interaction I had with Elaine from that point on was concerning the finances because we still had joint accounts. She didn't have the energy to separate the money, so we just periodically emailed to ensure that everything was square.

I did, however, write letters. Every day I would write Elaine a letter to share with her what was going on in me. Most of the letters were not blubbering or asking for forgiveness or begging; they were simply honest revelations of my heart. This was something that had not occurred before in our marriage due to my secrecy and lying. But God was truly changing my heart, softening me to the idea of what real manhood looked like. Because I did love Elaine, I wanted her to see these changes. As much as I wanted to be reconciled to Elaine, I didn't expect anything in return for the letters. I just wanted an outlet to share my thoughts and feelings.

The more letters I wrote the more I learned about myself, primarily how dishonest I had lived my life to that point. I was astonished at how easy it had become for me to lie. It was as natural as breathing. As my days of recovery and transformation turned into months, I was learning to tell the truth. That may appear odd to say that I was "learning" to tell the truth, but it was a process. Sexual addiction blinded me from seeing the truth plainly because my addiction was founded on lies. The more I ingested the lies the less able I was to see the plain truth. And as I formed the daily habit of lying to cover up my addictive behaviors it became easier to just lie about anything, even if I didn't have to. Learning to tell the truth was more painful than

I anticipated. It meant being honest about the ugliness of my sin, my secrets. It meant no more hiding. I was used to hiding. I believed it was safer to hide than to let the real me be seen. But truth-tellers don't cover up, they don't hide. And I knew I had to become a truth-teller if I was ever going to break free from my past, my addiction, and my secrets.

So, I committed to telling the truth, even as all the bumps of my recovery cropped up. I would tell my counselor and support group friends whenever I failed. I would share with them specifically the temptations I was facing throughout the week, not hiding or rationalizing or justifying them away. I began to share my honest emotions, even the negative ones. As painful as this process of learning to tell the truth was, it was powerful and liberating. As I heard one man put it, "When you tell the truth, that's all you have to remember."

But I was still separated from Elaine and this brought deep sadness to my recovery process. I prayed every night, and multiple times throughout the day, for Elaine. How I longed to go back and erase the past, changing the gross betrayals I had committed against her. I felt very conflicted during those first six months of my recovery. I was excited for what God was doing in changing me, but I was also grieving the loss of my dearest friend and lover. All I could do was offer up my sorrow and heartache to God, trusting that he would carry me (and Elaine) through.

Living in the Light

Do you believe God's grace truly is greater than all your sin, all your secrets? Is it difficult for you to embrace such grace? I can understand. We often believe there will come a point in our lives where we have gone too far, sinned too much for God to keep extending grace to us. But that is simply a misunderstanding of who God is and how deep and wide his love is for us. God's grace cannot be overwhelmed by our sin.

If you want to live in the light you must embrace God's grace. Come clean with him and thank him for his willingness to never let you go, no matter how far you have strayed. There is never a moment in which God is unwilling to receive a prodigal home.

But when you come home, when you set the secrets free and begin to live in the light, you must learn to be a truth-teller. The patterns of secrecy are broken through telling the truth. Get in the daily habit of keeping your life uncovered before those you love. No more secrets, no more lies, no more shame. Live in the light of truth and don't allow anything to be tucked back into the dark corners of your mind or heart. It may take some time to become skilled in this area, but it is worth the effort.

Blessings

I don't know if I will ever comprehend the mercy and grace of God. I know the wretch I have been (and still can be), yet God seems to prefer dealing with me out of his kindness. This amazes me to this day, and I expect it will amaze me for all eternity. It was God's limitless grace that ultimately restored my marriage.

Yes, God healed my marriage!

******

The end of a matter is better than its beginning.
(Ecclesiastes 7:8)

God gave me a promise near the beginning of my transformation process. It was contained in the above verse. The end of a matter is better than its beginning.

The beginning of my recovery was a mess, as I illustrated in the previous chapter. But God kept extending hope to me by encouraging me that what lay ahead was better than where I had been, or even was at the moment. He proved this to me when Elaine and I began to talk again.

After almost seven months of separation, Elaine was willing to have a conversation with me. It started small, a phone call here or me going over for a brief visit to her parents' house. These talks didn't focus on the future of our marriage as much as they were just times for us to gradually open up about what God was teaching us. I was amazed at the healing journey Elaine seemed to be on. I had just assumed that she was broken beyond repair, but I saw God healing her just as miraculously as he was transforming me.

In the spring of 2000, Elaine and I went on a date. I was nervous, even more nervous than our first date six years prior. I didn't want to blow this opportunity to treat Elaine as she deserved, as a woman of immeasurable value and beauty. But I also didn't want to come on too strong and make her feel uncomfortable, like I was forcing her to move toward me emotionally or romantically. So, we did the standard dinner and a movie date. It was a pleasant evening that went the way you might imagine a date should go. While there weren't any profound, earth-shattering decisions made, I felt hope, a strong feeling that God might just be about the business of resurrecting my lifeless marriage. But it was just one date.

******

By March, we were talking about getting back together. Elaine was nervous (so was I) but she could see that significant, genuine change was occurring in my life. The kind of change that can only be attributed to the miraculous grace of God. In faith, and with much prayer, we decided to give our marriage another shot.

On April 8, 2000, we went back to the church where we were first married. With our immediate families present, we restated our vows and marked a new beginning, a testament to the work of God's grace and healing in our lives. It was quite an emotional time for me in particular because I felt so undeserving of such incredible kindness and restoration. God's grace became living that day.

What impressed me the most on the day of our "remarriage" was the fact that my father-in-law prayed for us. His prayer was honest, even stating his feelings of hatred for me at the pain I had caused his little girl. But his prayer was also merciful and filled with hope and wonder at the miracle God was performing. I will cherish that prayer forever, for it revealed to me that God was restoring our entire family, not just my marriage.

After the ceremony, Elaine moved back into our house and we began the process of adjusting to our new life together. It was a joyful time, but certainly not devoid of some apprehensions and nervousness for both of us. I was still learning how to live a transparent life and Elaine was still healing from the wounds of broken trust and betrayal. But there was definitely a stark contrast from our old life together before. Our home now was filled with peace rather than anger and chaos. Our conversations were respectful and compassionate and purposeful. It was a whole new world and I liked it.

God was proving to me that the end of a matter is better than its beginning. I was not lonely anymore. God had given me back my best friend, my cherished lover, my beloved wife. I felt complete, and grateful for such a gift of grace. I couldn't imagine any greater blessing in my recovery.

******

"Aaahhhhhh!!!"

I could hear the screaming all the way out in the living room. I jumped up from my chair and ran to the back of the house where the screaming was coming from. Elaine was in the bathroom. I knocked on the door to see what was the matter.

"I'm pregnant!" she yelled from behind the closed door.

I had no idea how to react to such news. You would think I should have done backflips and skipped through the house, but this news came just weeks after Elaine and I had moved back in together. On one hand, I felt like I needed to console Elaine because of the stress that this news just added to her already fragile emotions. But, on the other hand, I was pumped!

Unlike earlier times in my life when I would have stuffed all my emotions, I instead shared them with Elaine, both the positive and negative feelings. We talked it out. Elaine shared how she was feeling divided about such news because there couldn't be anything more exciting than her being a mom, but she was also nervous because she felt there was so much uncertainty about the stability of our marriage because of my history. We agreed to take it one day at a time and ask God for the wisdom and strength to make it through that season in our lives.

As we went through the months leading up to the delivery, God revealed his nature in an unmistakable way. I was reading the Bible one day and came across the following passage.

> I will repay you for the years the locusts have eaten—
> the great locust and the young locust, the other locusts
> and the locust swarm—my great army that I sent
> among you. You will have plenty to eat, until you are
> full, and you will praise the name of the LORD your
> God, who has worked wonders for you; never again
> will my people be shamed. (Joel 2:25–26)

God was showing us in a tangible way that he is able to bring life from death. In our case, he was bringing an actual human life out of our seemingly dead marriage. And we were grateful, excited, and scared (like every new parents-to-be).

Haley was born on December 15, 2000, and was the most beautiful person I had seen in my whole life. Words will never describe the emotions I felt on that day. A real transformation was taking place in my life. I was able to feel, able to express my sense of thanksgiving and awe over the gracious gift of our baby girl.

In this vein of appreciation, we even gave our daughter a name that had significance. Haley means "hero." In my case, I couldn't think of a better word to describe God in my life.

God is my hero. He is the hero of my life, displaying his grace by rescuing me from the dungeon of secrecy, shame and addiction. He is the hero of my marriage, displaying his power by restoring our broken, lifeless relationship. He is the hero of my purpose, revealing his will by leading me, a broken sinner, into the ministry of helping others. The end of a matter is better than its beginning.

******

Three years into our new marriage, God began gently nudging me concerning what he wanted my future career to be. Unfortunately, I wasn't listening that closely. I was getting pretty comfortable in my new life. I was growing in my love for Elaine, I totally enjoyed being a dad (by now, Ethan had been born and Megan was on the way), and I was even "doing my part" to help other men by leading a weekly support group at my church. Life was good. I believed this was it concerning God's promise that "the end of a matter is better than its beginning." Actually, there was more, a lot more.

In January 2003, I got laid off from my job. This was unexpected, as I was in upper management at a national character education company. I had worked there for nearly five years and had even developed a close personal relationship with the president of the company. While the layoff was not personal, it was a difficult blow to take. But God was at work, even in the midst of me losing my job.

I wish I could tell you that I had developed such a close, personal intimacy with God at that time that I was completely in tune with what he wanted me to do in response to being laid off. But I can't tell you that because it would be a lie. I was just like anyone else who has lost a job, frantically polishing up my resume and calling everyone I knew who had any connections with personnel managers around town. In other words, I was taking action without actually consulting God on what my next move should be.

God, however, was patient and gracious with me (as he has always been throughout my life). During the next six months of hunting for a job (and coming up woefully empty), he was asking me a question in my private prayer times: "Jonathan, do you want unbelievable joy?" It seemed like an odd question considering my immediate circumstances of being jobless and a bit panicky about it.

But my response was simple, "Of course, who doesn't want unbelievable joy?"

"Then tell your story," was God's reply.

"What?! I'm not sure I heard you correctly."

"Do you want to experience unparalleled joy in your life?"

"Sure, of course I do."

"Then share your story of my healing in your life."

This inner conversation went on for several months before I realized that God was inviting me to embark on vocational ministry. He wanted me to share with others the indescribable gift he had been sharing with me. This calling was simultaneously exciting and terrifying. I wanted more than anything for others trapped in sexual addiction and a double life of secrets to experience the increasing level of happiness and freedom I was experiencing in my new walk with God. But I also didn't have a clue what such a ministry would look like in a practical sense. But I knew God was trustworthy and would not allow us to fail where he was leading.

In July 2003, Elaine and I founded Be Broken Ministries. We had no ministry experience, no training, no money, and no clue. But we did have God leading us and our story of redemption and healing. And this was all we needed. God has blessed our ministry and he has kept his promise too. I did not experience truly unparalleled joy until I began to give away my story, and the grace by which God rescued me, to others in need of rescue from their own secrets. My joy is multiplied by giving away what has been given to me.

God has shown me that he loves to bless his kids, not because of the things they do or don't do, but because he is madly in love with them. It has taken many years for me to embrace the truth that God is crazy about me—always. He is crazy about me when I'm doing right or doing wrong, when I'm up or when I'm down, when I feel his presence or when I don't. And he blesses at his own pleasure, even (or especially) when I don't deserve it.

The end of a matter is truly better than its beginning.

******

Of all the blessings God has given since that fateful Saturday back in 1999, possibly the greatest blessing of all has been the courage to be real, to be honest about who I am no matter what the consequences. It isn't always easy, or natural, for me to remain transparent and vulnerable, even with those I love the most. But the joy of being fully known and fully loved by my wife, my kids, and my friends is indescribable. My heart is finally at peace.

"With God all things are possible." (Matthew 19:26)

Living in the Light

Can you trust God that what is before you is better than what is behind you? This is called hope, to desire with expectation of fulfillment. God is good and he loves you more than anyone, and his desire for you is that you find total satisfaction

in him alone. Whatever secrets you are hiding, whatever dividedness you are experiencing in your life, any pain or abuse or
shame you carry, God can heal it. You may think it would be
impossible for your life to be free from shame or secrets or self,
but with God all things are possible.

One of my favorite verses in scripture is Psalm 37:4, "Take
delight in the LORD and he will give you the desires of your
heart." Are you finding your delight in the Lord? If you are living a double life I can guarantee you are not. So, why not take
a step of faith, trusting that God truly does have your best at
heart, and uncover the real you? Let God touch your heart and
speak promises of good things to come if you will only delight
yourself in him. He already sees all that you are hiding and he
is still madly in love with you. So, it is to your benefit to just
give up playing the game of secrets and experience a new life in
the light.

The Final Chapter

The final chapter of my life is not written…yet. Because of this I have many opportunities to mess it up. That's right. I could gather more secrets. I could tell more lies. I could hurt more people, even people I love dearly. But I also suppose that since my life isn't over yet, I have just as many opportunities to get it right, to swing for the fence and actually connect for a home run. So what will determine how my final chapter will read when the last pen stroke is written? Hard to tell. My hope is that it will read, "No more regrets."

I must admit that I have lived many regrettable moments. I regret the secrets I have carried, the lies I have told, the hearts I have broken, and the shame I have brought to the name of Christ. My history is littered with many mistakes, some out of ignorance, many more out of willful defiance. I am not proud of these moments, I grieve them. But I am learning from them, learning what it means to live in the now, unbound to the shame of my past or the questions of my future. Right now, this is life.

Life occurs in the moment, this moment. You can't live in the past. You can shackle yourself to the past, either wishing life was "as it was" or wallowing in the injustices that occurred against you. Either way, you lose. You miss this moment, you miss life.

It is just as useless to be too future-minded, always thinking about whatever is next. Tomorrow is not promised. To live there is to gamble away the moment you are given right now, and those stakes are high.

My journey to this point is teaching me that to wallow in my past or obsess over an unknown future is to forfeit real life, to give up my now. I don't want to miss life, the abundant life God wants me to have right now. I have made peace with my past by resting on the grace of God, I entrust my future to the One who knows the number of my days, and I press into this moment, engaging life unburdened by the weight of my secrets and shame. It feels good to walk with my chin up, not feeling a need to glance over my shoulder in guilt. I like freedom. I don't want to go back to the dark life of dividedness and fear. I want to live this moment without regret.

******

I wish I could say that I have it all together and that I have completely figured life out. I haven't. I am just like you. I am up, down, and sideways, often all in the same day—or hour. This is the nature of life. As I journey on, effectively writing the subsequent chapters of my life, I realize that the road to a full life is not flat. It seems to be primarily uphill and contain lots of obstacles and potholes. Sometimes there is no road at all, just a sign that reads, "Jump." But I am finding that with God in the lead I am given all I need to navigate the trail. I can make it to my destination, I can fulfill my purpose.

I remember one time I was playing with my kids in my bedroom. They were toddlers at the time. They were hopping all over the bed, laughing and having a great time. I was standing about three feet away from the bed, watching their antics, when all of a sudden my son jumped off the bed and lunged toward me. I wasn't expecting this, but I quickly turned and caught him. He giggled gleefully as I tossed him back onto the bed to continue playing. I was amazed at his uninhibited faith in me.

It never crossed his mind to doubt that I would catch him. He simply flung himself off the bed in my direction, as if it was all part of his enthusiastic playtime. That picture has stuck in my head of how I believe God wants my life to be. Enthusiastic faith, never doubting that God will catch me as I toss my life, with all its imperfections, his direction. No doubt, no fear, just simple, childlike faith. Oh, that my final chapter would contain such verses.

I am not a perfect man. I still struggle with keeping secrets. Granted, they aren't the nature of secrets I have kept in the past, but the temptation is still very real. And I don't always make the right choices, but I press on. I don't allow the secrets to remain hidden, to eat away at my life. No, I confess them and move in toward my relationships.

What seems most challenging for me in living a life without secrets is that life is so daily. Every day there are new thoughts, new conversations, new work, and new temptations. The uphill climb continues and my legs grow weary and my back bends. It often seems like it would just be so much easier to give in and hide a few secrets here and there. Not big ones, maybe just a few small ones, like not mentioning a second look or not sharing an envious thought of friends who own more stuff than I do. Day by day the challenges come, begging me to take the bait and hide the secrets. The challenges are tough, but I am ever reminded of where my secrets led me: death.

******

I have to confess, I do still have one secret. But I don't want to carry it anymore. I want to share it with you. It is the secret to true happiness. I know there are a lot of other people out there saying they have the secret to happiness, but how many of them are truly happy? I am truly happy, content in my relationships, joyful in my work, grateful for God's mercy. I want you to know what makes for a truly happy life, an abundant life. I want you to carry the one secret that is worth carrying.

Here it is:

Love God and love others with nothing hidden. Because when you live in the light, darkness (secrets) cannot overtake you.

No more regrets.

Living in the Light

What are you waiting for? Go live your life . . . in the light.

Appendix

BOOKS

Blue Like Jazz, Donald Miller
The Bondage Breaker, Neil T. Anderson
Can My Marriage be Saved?, Mae & Ericka Chambers
Every Man's Battle, Stephen Arterburn & Fred Stoeker
Healing Is a Choice, Stephen Arterburn
Healing the Wounds of Sexual Addiction, Mark Laaser
Jesus in the Margins, Rick McKinley
Knowledge of the Holy, A.W. Tozer
Man of Valor, Richard Exley
Messy Spirituality, Mike Yaconelli
Naked & Unashamed: Recapturing Family Intimacy, Bill Mills
This Beautiful Mess, Rick McKinley
Transforming Grace, Jerry Bridges
Victory Over the Darkness, Neil T. Anderson
When Lost Men Come Home, David Zailer
Winning the Battle Within, Neil T. Anderson

COUNSELORS

For help in finding good, qualified Christian counselors, contact the organizations below.

American Association of Christian Counselors (www.aacc.net) 1.800.526.8673
Bebroken.com Counselor Network (www.bebroken.com) 1.800.49.PURITY
Christian Counselors Directory (www.christiantherapist.com)
Focus on the Family (www.family.org) 1.800.A.FAMILY
New Life Ministries (www.newlife.com) 1.800.NEW.LIFE

SUPPORT GROUPS

SEXUAL ADDICTION GROUPS

Bebroken.com Support Group Network (www.bebroken.com)
1.800.49.PURITY
Celebrate Recovery (www.celebraterecovery.com)
Every Man's Battle Support Groups (www.everymansbattle.
com) 1.800.NEW.LIFE
LIFE Ministries (www.freedomeveryday.org) 1.866.408.LIFE
S-Anon International (www.sanon.org) 1.800.210.8141 Sexa-
holics Anonymous (www.sa.org) 1.866.424.8777

SUBSTANCE ABUSE GROUPS

Al-Anon Family Groups (www.al-anon.org) 1.888.4AL.ANON
Alcoholics Anonymous (www.aa.org) 212.870.3400
Alcoholics Victorious (www.alcoholicsvictorious.org)
Cocaine Anonymous (www.ca.org) 310.559.5833
Narcotics Anonymous (www.na.org) 818.773.9999

OTHER HELPFUL MINISTRIES

Be Broken Ministries (www.bebroken.com) Eternal
Perspectives Ministry (www.epm.org)
Focus on the Family (www.family.org)
Gateway to Freedom Workshops (www.gatewaymen.com)
Harvest USA (www.harvestusa.org)
Healing for the Soul (www.healingforthesoul.org)
Mastering Life Ministries (www.masteringlife.org)
National Coalition for the Protection of Children & Families
(www.nationalcoalition.org)
New Life Ministries (www.newlife.com)
Operation Integrity (www.operationintegrity.org)
Pure Life Ministries (www.purelifeministries.org)
Stone Gate Resources (www.stonegateresources.org)